Oracle Data Integrator

12c Developer
JUMPSTART GUIDE

Soundarapandian Murugarajan

Author : Mr. Soundarapandian Murugarajan

Editors : Ms. Vijayalakshmi Janakiraman & Ms. Sara Barack

Inspired by: Mr. Venkat Sankaran & Mr. Rajesh Sharma

August 2014: First Edition

<u>Dedicated To</u>

My Mentors: Mr. Ramji & Mr. Anantha Raman

My Wife Sumithra

My Son Suraj and Daughter Nila

1   Table of Contents

1　Preface

1.1　About The Author

Soundarapandian Murugarajan earned his Bachelor's degree in commerce and Master's Degree in Information Technology. He has over 20 years of experience in Information Technology using Oracle products. Mr. Murugarajan has worked on several projects to provide enterprise-wide solutions to implement ERP and Data warehouse solutions. He provides solutions to customers across the globe in countries such as America, Canada, Mexico, Chile, United Kingdom and India. He provides solutions to a variety of customers in multiple Industries such as Oil & Gas, Banking, Semiconductor, Transportation, and Automotive

2　This Book

2.1　About This Guide

The intention of this book is to provide a jumpstart for a developer to gain knowledge on how to do ELT using Oracle Data Integrator 12c. This book explains the most common business requirements using a simple source and target objects. This manuscript contains real time examples with step-by-step guidance and screenshots.

All examples used are simple in nature. The idea is for the reader to gain confidence with using the Oracle Data Integrator. Examples are intended to be a good encouraging factor for developers to gain confidence. This book is designed to be a stepping-stone for the developer to venture into advance features of Oracle Data Integrator. After reading this book, developers are meant to gain a basic idea on how to use Oracle Data Integrator during their development cycle.

Just by reading the ODI developer guide, a developer may not be able to perform mapping, however the step-by-step screen shots provided in this book will enable the developer to understand the tool better.

There are other ways to perform the ELT other than the ones explained in this book. The intent of this guidebook is to show a sample method only. Developers can feel free to try their own methods to accomplish their results.

Below are examples that were used to explain the Oracle Data Integrator:

> Source to Target – Append data
> Source to Target - Incremental update
> Using Join in Mapping
> Using Lookups in Mapping
> Using Union in Mapping
> Using Reusable Mapping in Mapping **(New 12c feature)**
> Using Split in Mapping **(New 12c feature)**
> Using Markers in ODI
> Flat file to Table upload
> ODI Packages
> ODI Procedures
> Load Planner

In the author's opinion, the ROI for buying this book will be over 100% because this guide is proven to save valuable time when learning ETL using Oracle Data Integrator 12c. In general it may take a Developer two to three weeks to understand and begin ETL coding. With the help of this guide, a developer can start coding in a very short period of time; perhaps in three to four days time.

2.2   Intended Audience

This book is intended for Developers who are one of the following:

1. New to Oracle Data Integrator
2. Have knowledge of other ETL tools such as Informatica, Ab-Initio, and Data Stage and want to develop ELT using Oracle Data Integrator

2.3   How to use this book

To get the most out of this book follow and perform the steps below.

2.3.1   Install Oracle Database

You must install Oracle database. Please refer to Oracle Data Integration certification mapping.

http://www.oracle.com/technetwork/middleware/ias/downloads/fusion-certification-100350.html

In this book we are using Oracle version 12.1.0.1.0.

```
SQL*Plus: Release 12.1.0.1.0 Production on Mon Jul 14 19:35:56 2014
Copyright (c) 1982, 2013, Oracle.  All rights reserved.
```

2.3.2   Install Oracle Data Integrator

Download and install Oracle Data Integrator 12c

In this book we are using Oracle Data Integrator version 12.1.2.

2.3.3   Database Preparations

Create tables, sequences using Database Objects Creation Scripts as per steps provided in this book.

2.3.4   Oracle Data Integrator Preparations

Perform Topology Setup as per steps provided in the 'Topology Setup' section.
Perform Designer Setup as per steps provided in the 'Designer Setup' section.

www.odijumpstart.com

3   ODI Overview

Oracle Data Integrator performs data transformation/validation using below steps.

      Extract
      Load
      Transfer

Traditional tools are used to do Extract, Transfer and Load i.e. ETL. But, ODI uses ELT. The advantage of ELT is that data gets moved from the Source system on an as is basis, without adding extra load to the Source system. Heavy-duty validation and transformation happens in the ODI server. This will enable ODI to handle large sets of data. As data grows, it can be made scalable to meet the growth.

3.1   ODI Architecture and Components

3.2   What is ELT?

ELT means Extract data from source, Load data into staging area, and perform Transformation as required.

3.2.1   Extract

In this step, the data gets extracted from one or more source systems running on different operating systems and databases. The Operating system can be Windows Server, UNIX, Linux etc., the database can be a SQL server, Oracle, Flat File, Excel spreadsheet etc.,

3.2.2   Load

In this step, extracted data gets loaded into a data warehouse. In general it gets loaded into a staging area for further validations.

3.2.3   Transform

In this step, the extracted data gets validated to ensure that the downstream reporting will be accurate. During this step, surrogate keys get assigned to the records.

4   ODI Studio Overview

In this section you will learn to know the different components of Oracle Data Integrator (ODI).

4.1   Designer

This is the most frequently used component of Oracle Data Integrator used by Developer. Developer uses this section to define Projects, Models, ETL Mappings, Variables, Knowledge base, Load Plan etc., Work repository stores the Designer metadata.

The Designer Navigator consists of the following sections:

> Projects
> Models
> Load Plans and Scenarios
> Global Objects
> Solutions

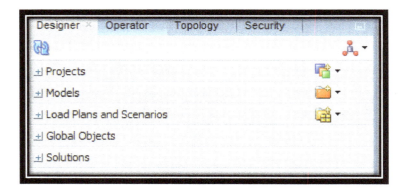

4.1.1   Projects

This section of the Oracle Data Integrator enables Developer to create, Project specific folders. All Variables and Knowledge modules defined with a Project are private to its Project only. As soon as a Project folder gets created, it will create the below sub-sections by default.

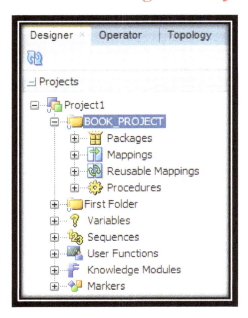

4.1.1.1   Packages

The ODI packages are used to group multiple ODI objects such as Variable, Mapping, and Procedures in a specific sequence of execution. Using Packages, one can evaluate True or False and take a different path based on the User's need. Package is a diagrammatic representation of Jobs. The workflow of Jobs gets defined by drag and drop scenarios.

4.1.1.2   Mappings

Mapping is an interface which consists of Source and Target with validation logics built in. The core logic of ETL is defined in the mapping section.

4.1.1.3   Reusable Mappings

Reusable mappings are similar to regular mapping. In addition to mapping, Reusable mapping can be used with a mapping. Reusable mapping has both Input and Output parameters.

4.1.1.4   Procedures

Procedure is a performing logic, which is not suitable for ETL Mapping. Even though Procedure can be used to validate and transform data, ETL mapping should be the first choice to do data validation and transformations. Procedure will support multiple technologies such as Operating System command, FTP, JMS command etc., ODI Procedures can be called with in an ODI Package. ODI Procedure can have more than one set of commands. Multiple commands are processed sequentially. A Procedure consists of commands from multiple technologies.

4.1.1.5   Variables

A variable is similar to variables in any programming language. The value can be set using a Select statement during the runtime. Oracle Data Integrator provides a feature to define static variables. The variable type can be Alphanumeric, Text, Numeric and Date. The Variables can be used in ETL mapping, Packages, Procedures.

4.1.1.6   Sequences

Sequences enable users to automatically generate sequence numbers with a specific incremental value. Sequence can be an ODI sequence or it can be based on a database. The sequence can be used in ETL mapping.

4.1.1.7   User Functions

User functions are used to create Project/System specific custom functions. It can be defined at a Project level or at a Global level. The ODI function can be used in ODI Mapping and ODI Procedures. User functions enable easy maintenance of commonly used functions.

4.1.1.8   Knowledge Modules

A Knowledge Module is a set of generic code that performs a specific task. KM uses ODI specific syntax to reference variables. Oracle provides several out of the box KM to enable faster development of ETL Mappings. Once defined in the KM, it can be used in multiple ETL mappings. KM can handle multiple technologies.

4.1.1.9   Markers

Marker is used to flag ODI objects. This will enable ODI objects to be grouped. Oracle provides 3 out of the box markers as shown below:

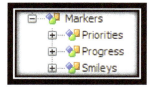

User can create custom Markers based on their needs.

4.1.2   Models

Model stores the structure of Source and Target objects such as Table, Files. Unless it is defined in the Model, the objects cannot be used in ETL mapping. Database table structure can be added to the Model using reverse engineering. Model does not store any data. It stores the structure of the object only. Using Model, data can be queried. Model can be used to add additional constraints to the objects, other than defined in the database.

4.1.3   Load Plans and Scenarios

The Load planner is used to execute ODI packages, ODI Procedures and ETL mapping in a serial or parallel manner. Load planner is used to populate data warehouse by running ODI jobs at specific intervals. Load planner stores the ODI job run times and session ID. Variables can be set during the execution of Load planner. Load planner also handles exception handling. Load planner has the capability to restart ODI jobs in multiple ways. Individual steps in the Load Planner can be enabled or disabled based on the user's need. Load Planner metadata is stored in work repository.

4.2   Operator

Use the Operator section is used to monitor the ETL jobs. After executing a scenario, a job can be monitored thoroughly in the Operator section. Operator has the flexibility of locating a Job by Date, Agent, Session, Status, Keyword and User.

The Operator Navigator consists of the following sections:

>   Session List
>   Hierarchical Sessions
>   Load Plans and Scenarios
>   Scheduling
>   Load Plan and Scenarios
>   Solutions

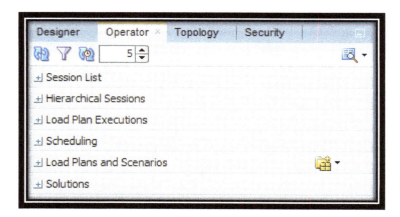

4.2.1   Session List

This section, shows the progress of running Jobs and the results of all completed Jobs. Once an ETL or Load plan is submitted for execution, its status can be monitored. The status of all ETL mappings can be viewed by Date, Agent, Sessions, Status, Keyword and User

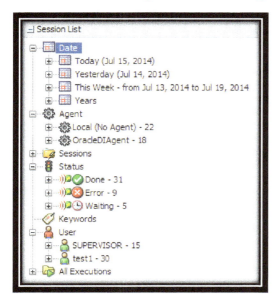

4.2.2　Hierarchical Sessions

Hierarchical session is similar to Session List but it shows Child sessions.

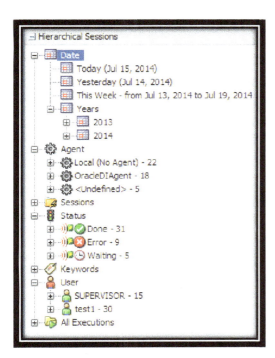

4.2.3   Load Plans and Scenarios

This section is specific to monitoring execution of Load plans.

4.2.4   Scheduling

This section shows all scheduled Load Plans by Agent and all scheduled jobs.

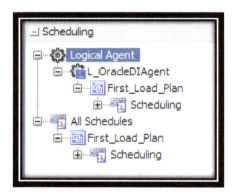

4.2.5   **Load Plan and Scenarios**

This section lists all available Load plans and Scenarios.

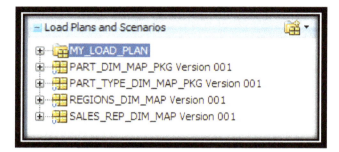

4.3   Topology

Topology is part of a Master repository. Using Topology navigator, you can manage the sever connection, database connection, physical and logical connections etc.,
Topology information is shared by Designer during the ETL mapping.

Topology has the below sub-sections

> Physical Architecture
> Contexts
> Logical Architecture
> Languages
> Repositories
> Generic Action

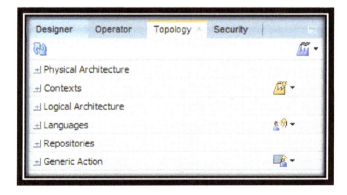

4.3.1   **Physical architecture**

In this section of the ODI, the physical characteristics of the environment can be defined. In this section, the server connection using ip address, server name can also be defined. Provide User name and password to login to Servers. The physical connection also defined by the type of database used during the connection.

The physical connection to a server is stored in Data server. A Data server can connect to one technology only. One data server can have multiple physical schemas.

Physical Agents are also defined in this section.

List of Technologies available are:

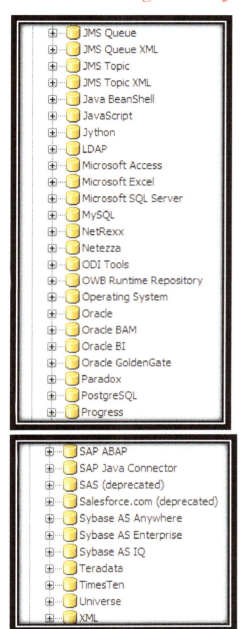

4.3.2   Logical architecture

The logical architecture is an alias to the Physical architecture. All data models within Oracle Data Integrator are built based on logical architecture. The great advantage of this approach is that it enables the same set of ETL to run on multiple environments by not changing any underlying code. As for as ETL mapping is concerned, change in Physical architecture connections will not have any impact on Export and Import of ETL mapping. Logical connection information gets transferred from one environment to another. Keeping a one-to-one relationship between physical and logical architecture will make the maintenance of Oracle Data Integrator easy.

4.3.3   Contexts

Contexts connect the Physical architecture and logical architecture together for usage with the Oracle data integrator. Using the Context, ETL mapping can be executed in different environments such as Development, Test and Production. This provides the flexibility of running ETL without installing a separate ODI in each environment.

GLOBAL context gets created by default.

4.3.4   Languages

In this section, you can see the available Programming languages and its commands available in the expression editor during the ETL mapping.

List of available languages are:

4.3.5   Repositories

In this section, Oracle data integrator repositories are listed. You can get details of Master and Work repositories.

4.4   Security

The Security section of Oracle Data Integrator will manage User access. In order to access ODI a User account is a must.

This section contains 3 main sub-sections as shown below:

        Profiles
        Users
        Objects

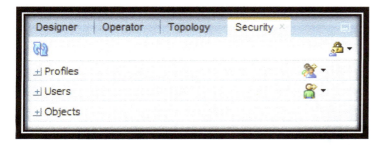

4.4.1   Profiles

ODI comes with the pre-build Profiles shown below. Every User account must have a CONNECT Profile along with other required profiles.

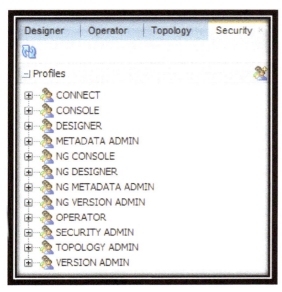

4.4.2   Users

In order for a User to login to ODI, an account needs to be created for the User. Assign Profiles to the User based on your requirements. User access to the ODI can be very specific to an Object level. In case of multiple Projects in ODI, User can be restricted to one or more specific projects. Users can also be restricted to specific task. For example, User can be allowed to run Load plan only, develop mapping only etc.

4.4.3   Objects

ODI comes with pre-build Objects level security. New Profiles can be created by allowing Objects into the Profile. User specific security can be built by allowing a specific Object to a Profile and assigning that Profile to the User.

4.5   Startup and Login

4.5.1   Startup Screen

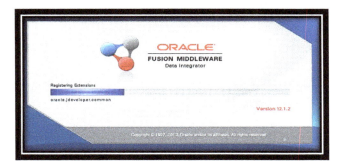

4.5.2   Login Screen

To Login, Click on Connect to Repository

Enter your User id and Password to login

4.6   Navigation Menu

5   Sample Database

In all examples, ELT interfaces are using two schemas. They are Source schema and Target schema.

NOTE: Please refer to Appendix A - Database Creation Script to create below database Objects

---

5.1   Source Schema Objects

Source schema consists of the Tables below:

5.1.1   Tables

Below are the lists of tables used in this book:

1. PARTS - Part Master table to store all parts
2. PART_TYPES - Parts Type table to store type of Parts.
3. CUSTOMERS - Customer master to store Customer data
4. REGIONS - Region list to report based on region
5. SALES_REPS - Sales person details
6. SALES_HEADERS - Sales header information
7. SALES_DETAILS - Sales detail information

5.1.2   **Source Schema ER Diagram**

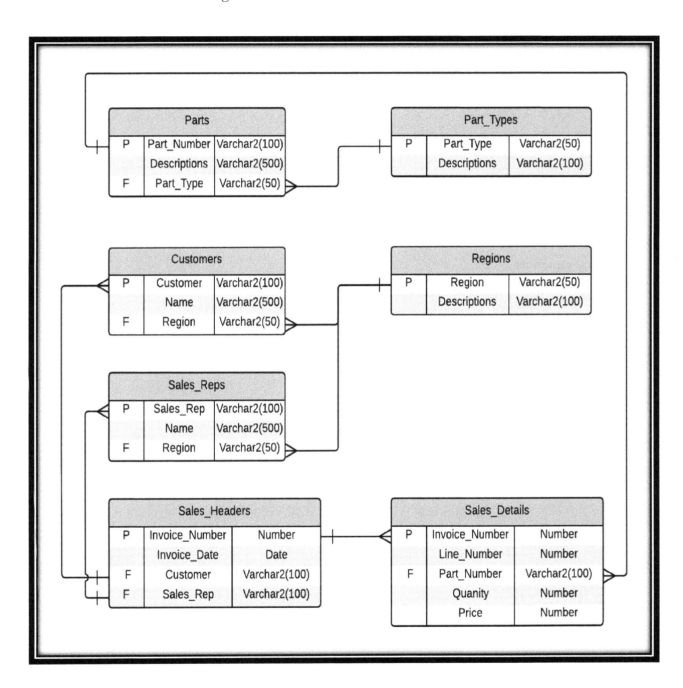

5.2 Target Schema Objects

Target schema consists of below Tables and Sequences.

5.2.1 Tables

Below are the lists of tables used in this book:

1. PARTS_DIM - Part Master table to store all parts
2. PART_TYPES_DIM - Parts Type table to store type of Parts.
3. CUSTOMERS_DIM - Customer master to store Customer data
4. REGIONS_DIM - Region list to report based on region
5. SALES_REPS_DIM - Sales person details
6. SALES_FACT - Sales information

5.2.2 Sequences

Below are the lists of sequences used to create surrogate key

1. PARTS_DIM_S
2. PART_TYPES_DIM_S
3. CUSTOMER_DIM_S
4. REGIONS_DIM_S
5. SALES_REPS_DIM_S
6. SALES_FACT_S

5.2.3   **Target Schema ER Diagram**

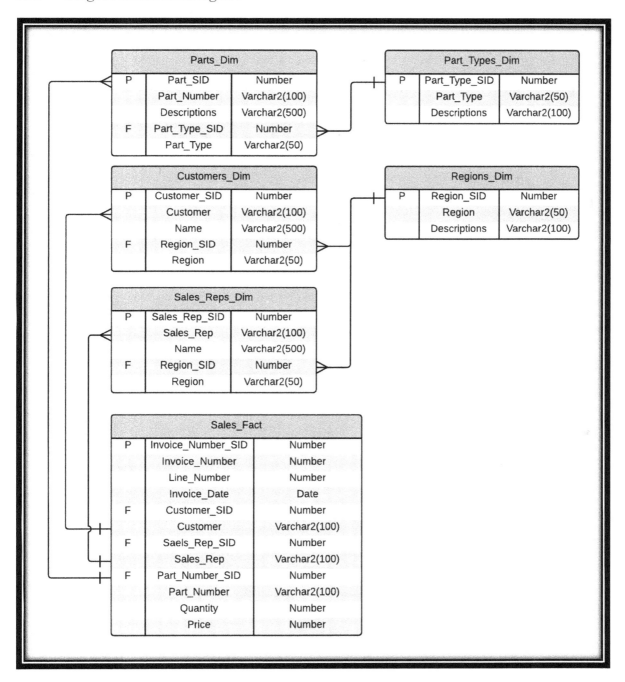

6 Topology Setup

6.1 Physical Schema

In this step you will create physical schemas for Source and Target.

Go to Topology

Expand Technologies

Expand Oracle

Right Click on 'Oracle' and Click on 'New Data Server'

Create Book Source Connection as shown below. Click on 'Test connection' to ensure that the connection is working.

6.1.1   Data Server - Book Source

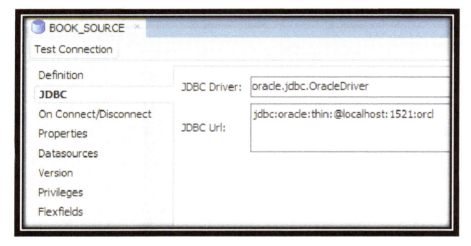

NOTE: Test connection by clicking on 'Test Connection' button.

6.1.2   Data Server - Book Target

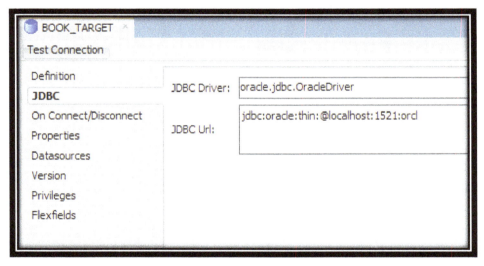

NOTE: Test connection by clicking on 'Test Connection' button.

6.2   Logical Schema

In this step you will create physical schemas for Source and Target.

Go to Topology -> Logical Architecture

Expand Technologies

Expand Oracle

Right Click on 'Oracle' and Click on 'New Logical Schema'

6.2.1   Logical Schema - Book Source

6.2.2   Logical Schema - Book Target

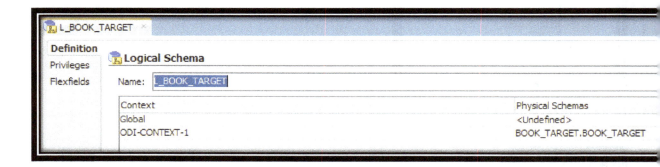

7   Designer Setup

In this section you will import the table structure from database. It will be used in the ELT mapping.

7.1   Model Setup

Go to 'Designer'

Expand 'Models'

Click on 'New Model Folder'

7.1.1   Model Folder - Book Source

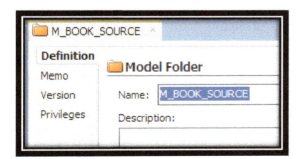

Save

You will see 'M_BOOK_SOURCE' folder created as shown below

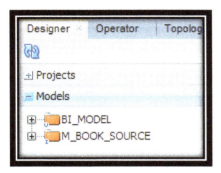

Right-Click on 'M_BOOK_SOURCE' and click on 'New Model'

Create Book source Model. Be sure to click:

Technology -> Oracle
Logical Schema -> L_BOOK_SOURCE

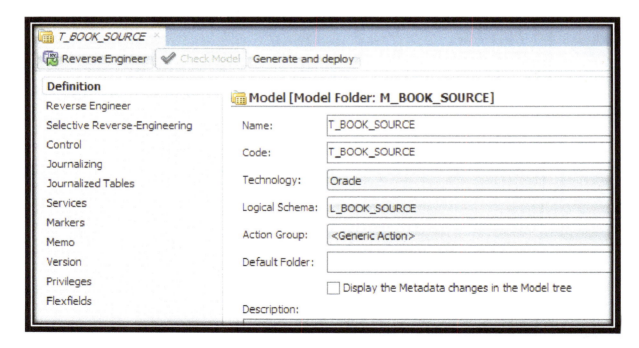

Save

This will create T_BOOK_SOURCE as shown below:

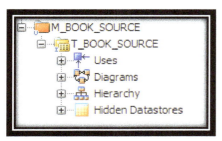

Click on 'Reverse Engineer'

To import all Table structures, select 'Standard', check 'Table' and enter % for Mask as shown below

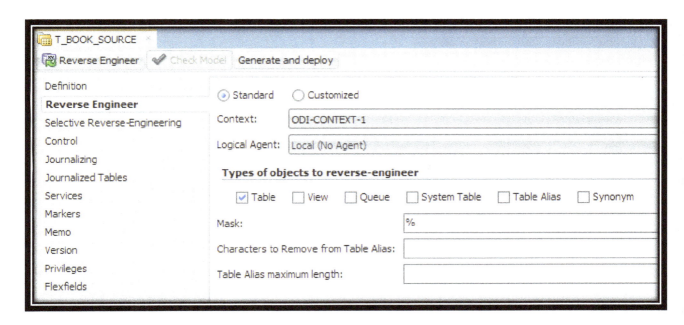

Click on 'Reverse Engineer' to extract the table structure from the database.

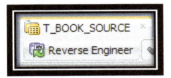

After Table structure extraction, ODI will create table structure as follows:

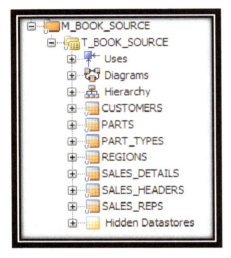

7.1.2   **Model Folder - Book Target**

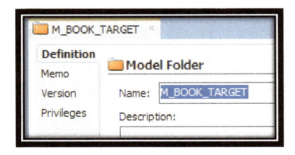

Save

You will see 'M_BOOK_TARGET' folder created as shown below:

Right-Click on 'M_BOOK_TARGET' and click on 'New Model'

Create Book source Model. Be sure to click:

Technology -> Oracle
Logical Schema -> L_BOOK_SOURCE

Save

This will create T_BOOK_TARGET as shown below:

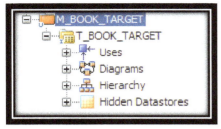

Click on 'Reverse Engineer'

To import all Table structures, select 'Standard' check 'Table' option and enter % for Mask as shown below

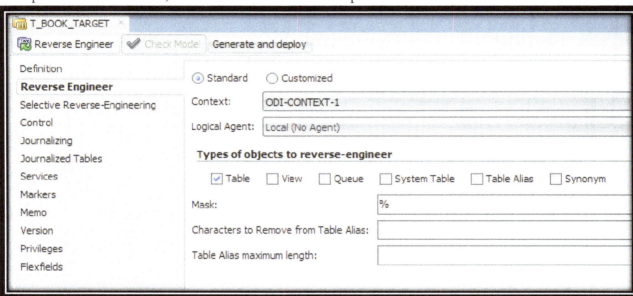

Click on 'Reverse Engineer' to extract the table structure from the database.

After Table structure extraction, ODI will create table structure as follows:

www.odijumpstart.com

7.2   Projects Setup

Go to Projects

Create a new Project with right click and choose 'New Folder'

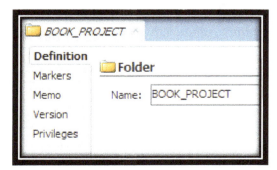

Save the Project

7.3   Sequence Setup

7.3.1   PART_TYPE_DIM_S Sequence

Go to 'Sequence'

Right click and select 'New Sequence'

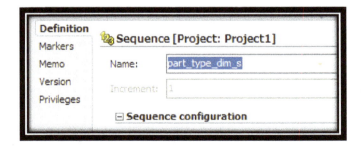

Click on 'Native Sequence'

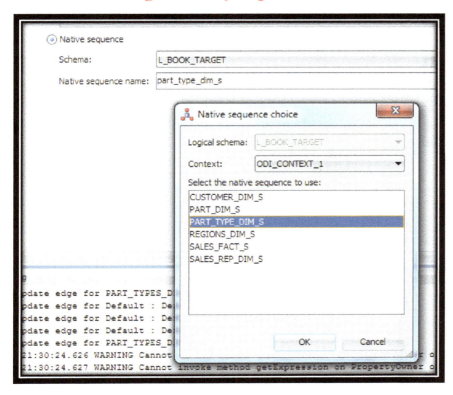

Click 'OK'

This will create the native sequence below:

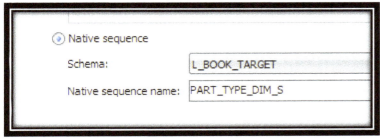

Create additional Sequences as shown below:

7.4   Import Knowledge Modules

Go to 'Knowledge Modules' and expand

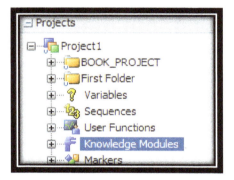

Click 'Integration (IKM)' then right click, and select 'Import Knowledge modules'

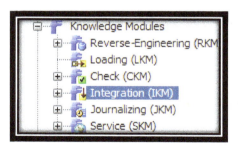

Oracle Data Integrator 12c Jumpstart Guide   P a g e | 38

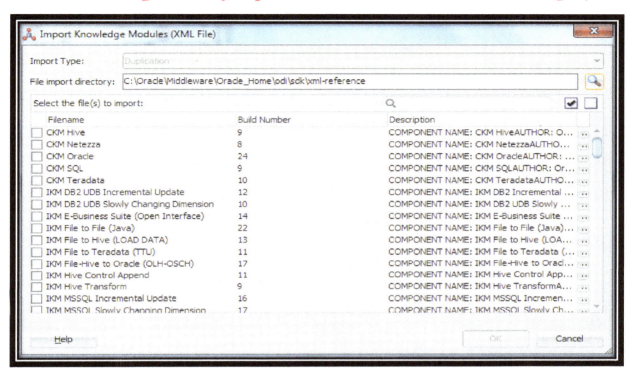

Select all required 'Knowledge Modules'. For this book we need the Knowledge Modules below:

1. IKM Oracle Incremental Update
2. IKM SQL Control Append
3. LKM SQL to Oracle
4. CKM Oracle

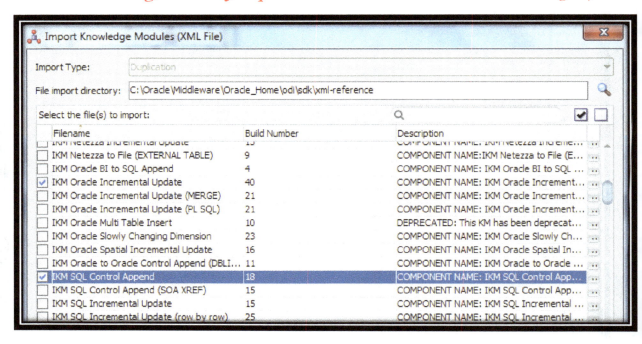

You will get below import report; make sure that no error reported.

New Knowledge Modules added as shown below

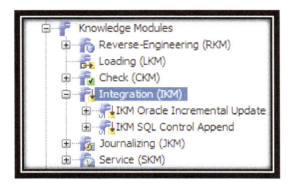

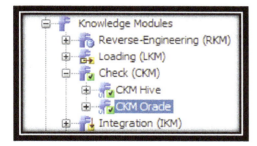

8   ETL Append Data

8.1   Append Data

In this example we are going to move data from the Source. Part_Types table to the Target.Part_Types_Dim

Create a new mapping by right clicking on 'Mapping' and then click on 'New Mapping'

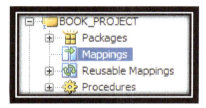

Create a New mapping called 'PARTY_TYPE_DIM_MAP'

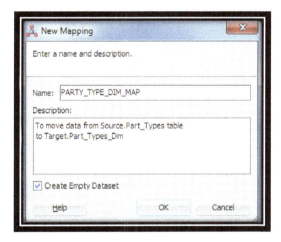

Click 'OK'

Drag and Drop 'PART_TYPES' to Source Area.

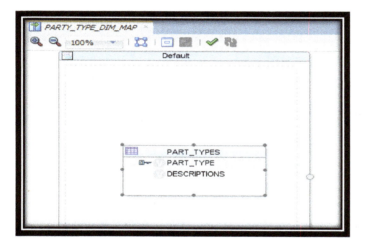

Drag and Drop Target table 'PART_TYPES_DIM'

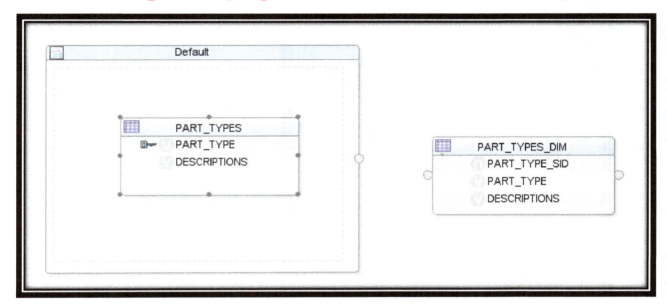

Connect PART_TYPES and PART_TYPES_DIM as shown below

Select the above connector and right click

Click 'Redo Attribute Matching ...'

Click 'OK' to automatically mapping source and target columns

Click on 'PART_TYPE_DIM.PART_TYPE' to check the mapping

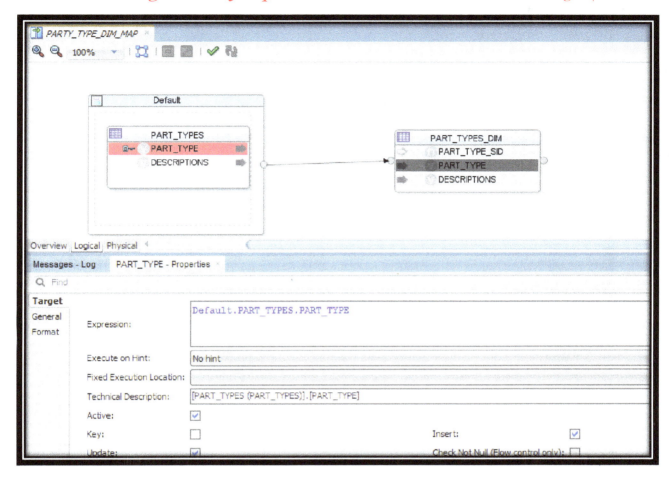

As you can see in the diagram above, the PARTS_TYPES_DIM.PART_TYPE get populated with PART_TYPES.PART_TYPE

Click on 'DESCRIPTION' to check the mapping.

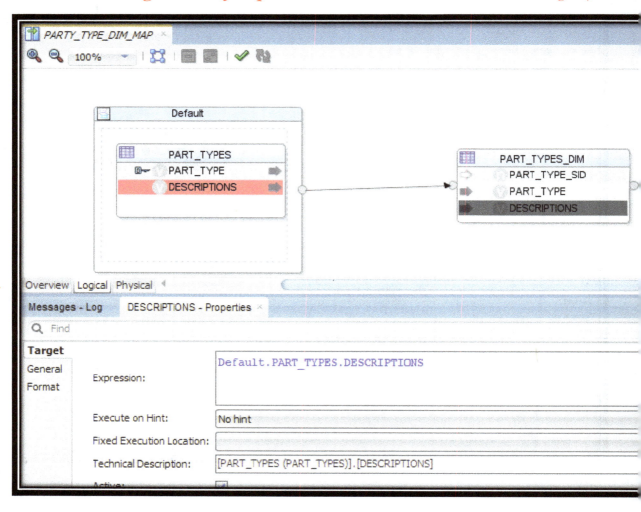

Let us populate PART_TYPE_SID with a sequence number.

Click on 'PART_TYPE_SID' and go to 'Property Window'

Click on 'Expression Editor'

You will get the screen below. Expand 'Project Sequence'

Drag and drop PART_TYPE_DIM_S sequence.

Click 'OK'

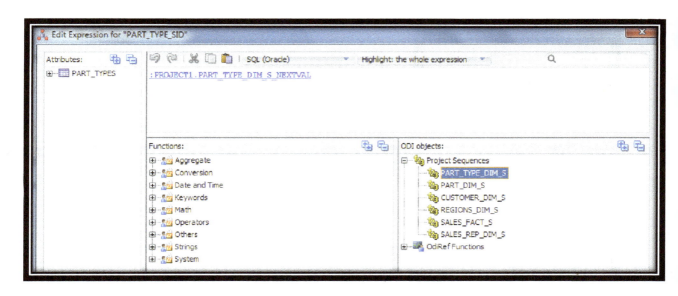

You will notice the sequence get validated and 'Technical Description' populated.

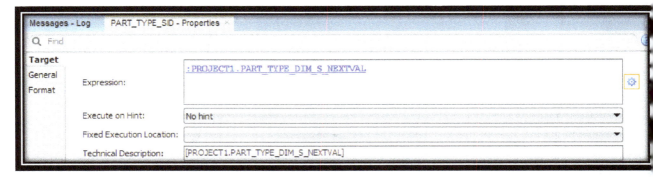

Make it a key, by checking 'Key'.

The Property window will be as shown below:

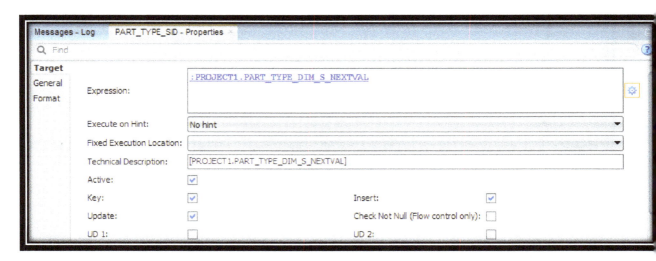

Go to Physical, to assign knowledge module to the ELT

Click on 'Physical'

You will get the below screen:

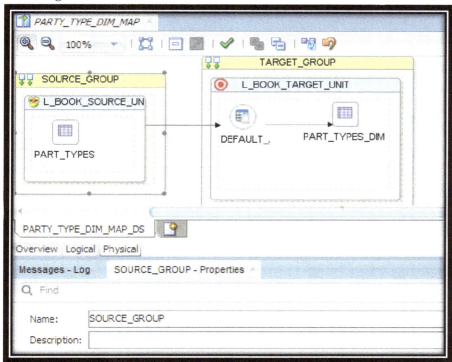

Click on the 'Default' icon.

Under the Properties window, click on 'Loading Knowledge Module'

Pick 'LKM SQL to Oracle'. You will see the screen below:

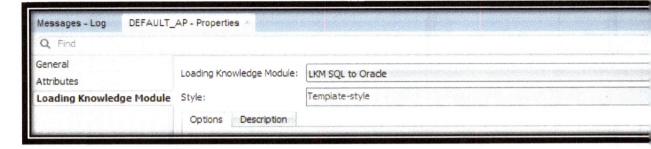

Click on 'PART_TYPES_DIM' to set up knowledge module.

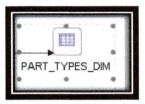

Click on 'Integration Knowledge Module' and select 'IKM SQL Control Append'

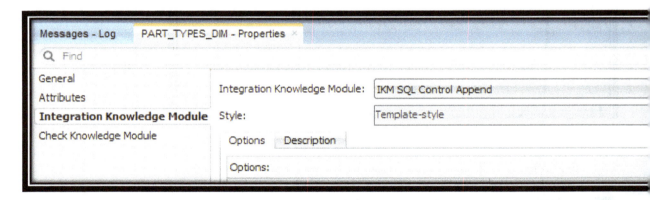

You can change the behavior of the knowledge module by turning on/off below properties. At this time, let us acquire the default values.

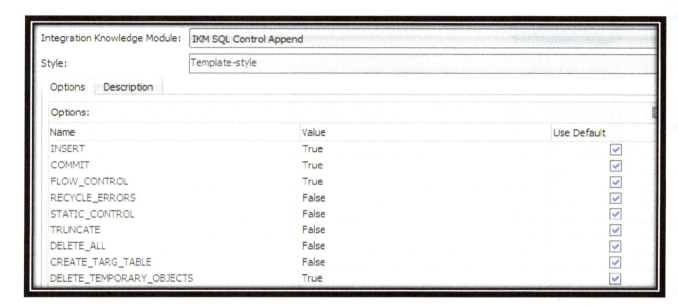

Click on 'Check Knowledge Module' and pick 'CMK Oracle' as shown below:

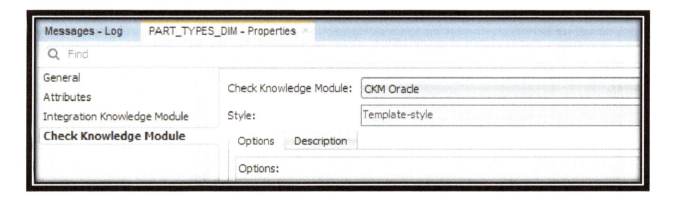

Save the ELT

Run the ELT by clicking 'Run' icon

Click 'OK'

You will see below screen showing 'Session Started':

To monitor the Job, go to 'Operator'

Expand 'Date' and you can see the Job completed successfully.

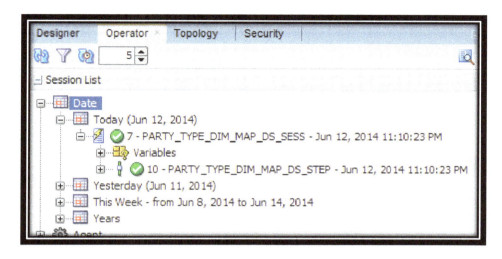

8.2   Results

As you can see below, 3 records were added to the table. Each record is assigned with a unique sequence number based on PART_TYPE_DIM_S sequence.

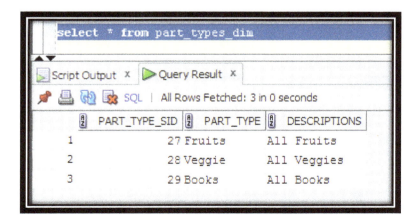

9 Incremental Upload

In this example, we are going to show you how to do an incremental update. This means, add a new record and update an existing record in case of any changes to the record.

We are going to move new / modified data from the Source.Part_Types table to the Target.Part_Types_Dim

9.1 Data set

9.1.1 Source

As you can see below, a new record added Record#4 and one record modified Record#1:

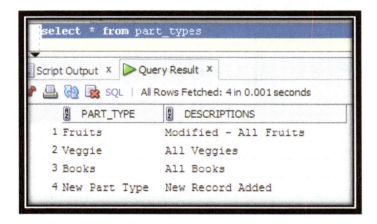

9.1.2 Target

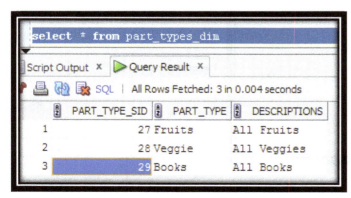

9.1.3   Expected Result

In the Target, one record will be added and one record will be updated.

9.2   Mapping

Create a new mapping by right clicking on 'Mapping' and then click on 'New Mapping'

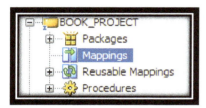

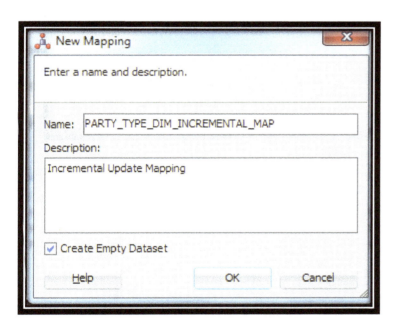

Click 'OK'

Drag and drop PART_TYPE to Source.
Drag and drop PART_TYPES_DIM to target as shown below:

For PART_TYPE_SID, Map the PART_TYPE_DIM_S sequence.

Enable only the 'Insert' option. Do not enable 'Update'.

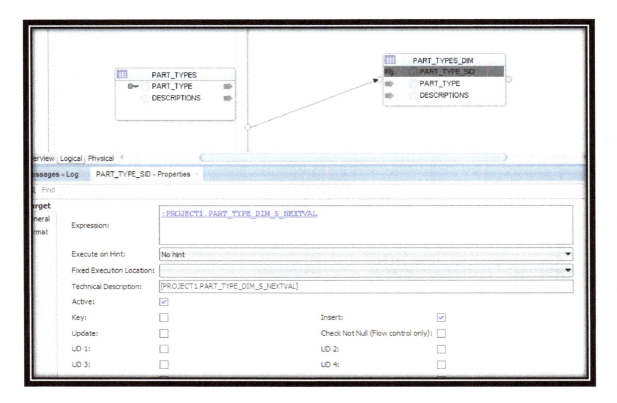

Define Part_Type as Key, by checking 'Key' as shown below.

Enable only the 'Insert' option. Do not enable 'Update'.

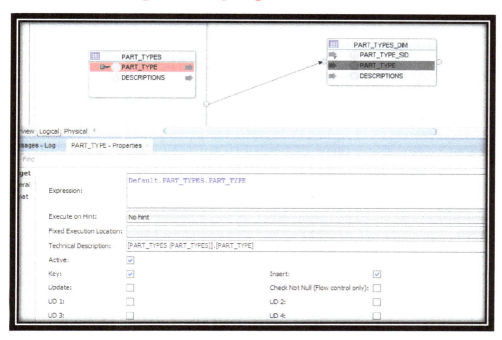

For 'DESCRIPTION' Property to Insert and Update. This option will enable ELT to update the change in Description.

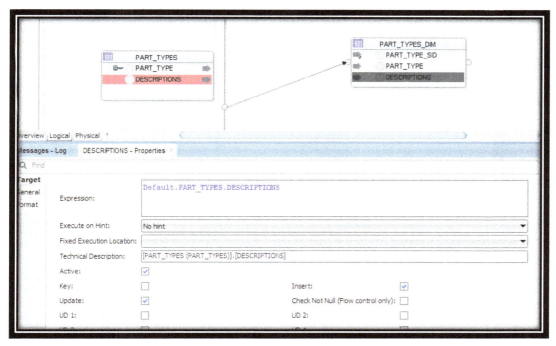

To setup Target type, Click on 'PART_TYPES_DIM'

Set 'Target' to Incremental Update as shown below:

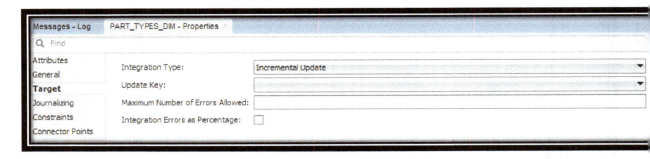

Go to 'Physical'

Click on 'Default' and make 'LKM SQL to Oracle' as 'Loading Knowledge Module'

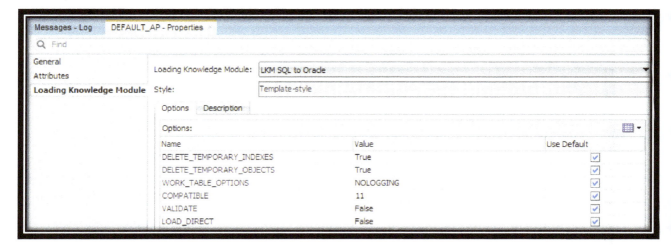

Click on 'PART_TYPES_DIM'

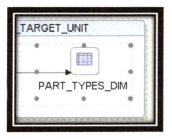

Click on 'Integration Knowledge Module' and pick 'IKM Oracle Incremental Update' knowledge module

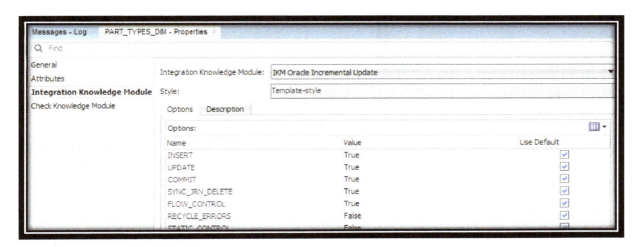

Click on 'Check Knowledge Module' and make sure the check knowledge module is 'CKM Oracle'

Save the ELT

Run the ELT

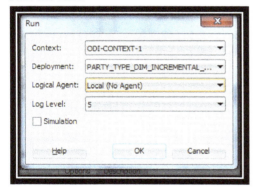

ELT successfully run as shown below:

9.3   Actual Result

As expected, one new record 'New Part Type ' added and 'Fruits' description updated.

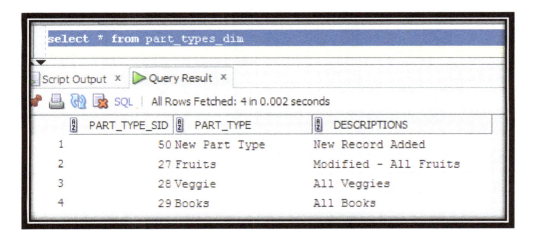

10 ELT using Lookup Tables

10.1 Data Set

10.1.1 Source

As part of this ELT, we are going to move the source data below to target. During the ELT process, we are going to do a look up to TARGET.PART_TYPE_DIM table and get the PART_TYPE_SID.

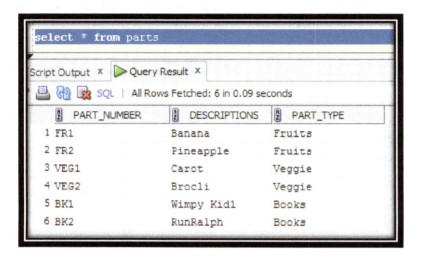

10.1.2 Target

The target table is empty now. After the ELT, all 6 records from the Source will be populated to the target table.

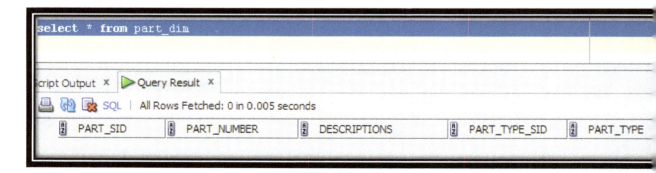

10.1.3 Expected Result

The target table is empty now. After the ELT, all 6 records from the Source will be populated to the target table.

10.2 Mapping

Create a new mapping by right clicking on 'Mapping' and then click on 'New Mapping'

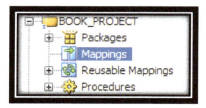

Click 'OK'

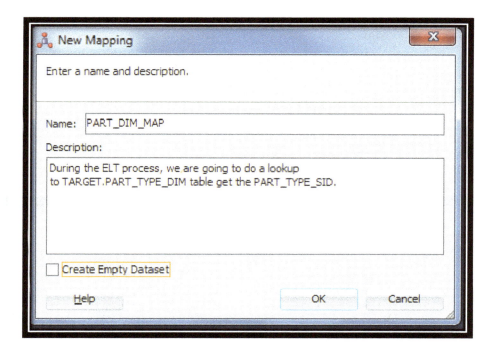

NOTE: This time we are creating an Empty Dataset

Drag and drop PARTS, PART_TYPE_DIM, PARTS_DIM as shown below:

www.odijumpstart.com

Now we are going to learn how to do lookup.

Drag and drop the lookup into the mapping as shown below:

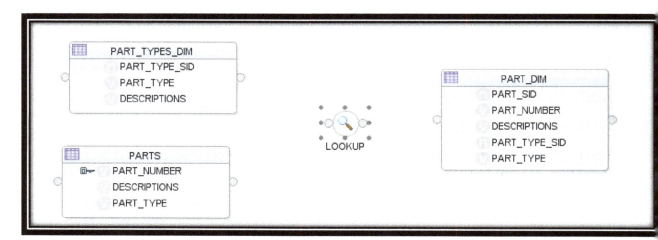

Drag and drop PART_TYPE from PARTS and PART_TYPE from PART_TYPES_DIM to LOOKUP

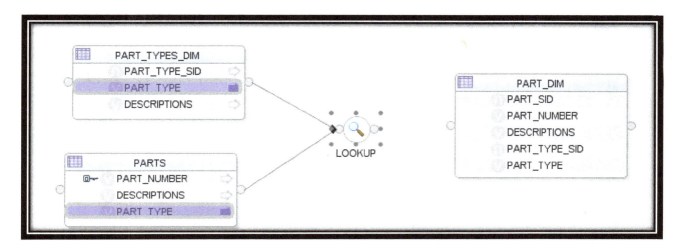

Click on 'LOOKUP' to see the lookup condition.

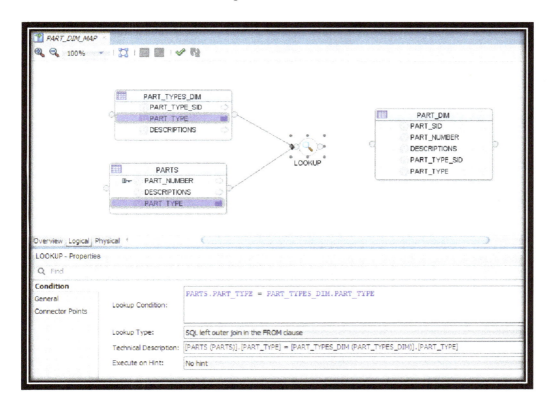

Drag and drop Source to Target as shown below:

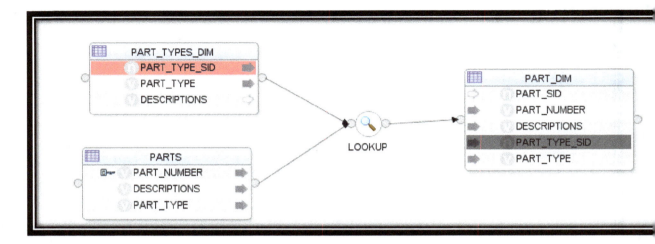

Click on 'LOOKUP' and click on 'Connector Point' to view the Input and Output connection points.

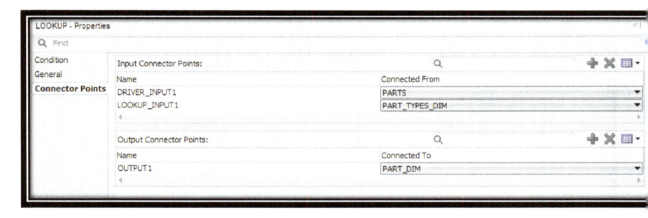

Click on Condition and pick 'Lookup Type' as SQL expression in the SELECT Clause.

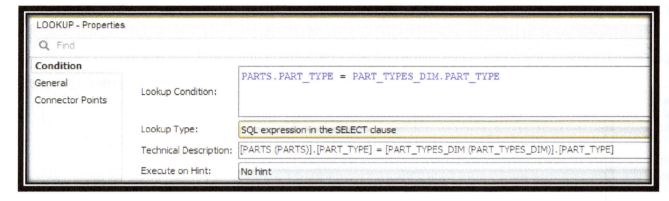

Click on 'PART_DIM' and make sure the 'Target' is Control Append.

For PART_SID, Map the PARTS_DIM_S sequence.

Click on 'PART_SID'. Go to Expression Editor and assign PARTS_DIM_S sequence.

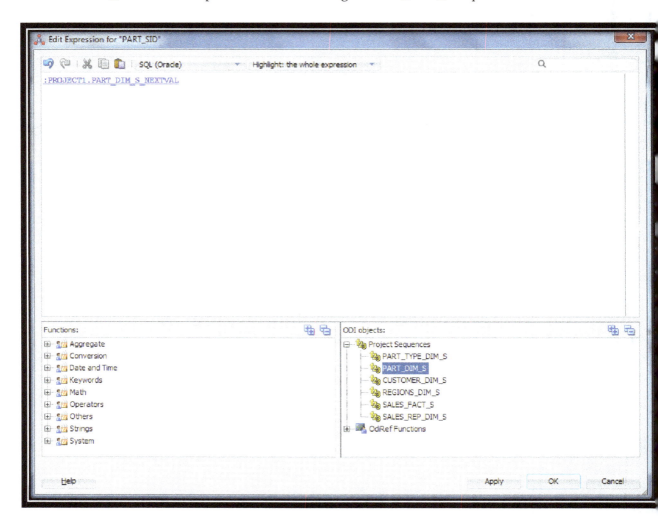

Enable only the 'Insert' option. Do not enable 'Update'.

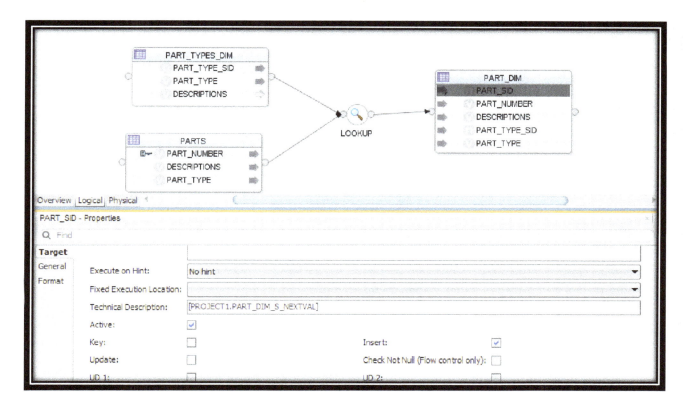

Save the ELT

Run the ELT

10.3 Actual Result

The result is as expected, All 6 records from the Source moved to Target. PART_TYPE_SID got populated using the lookup.

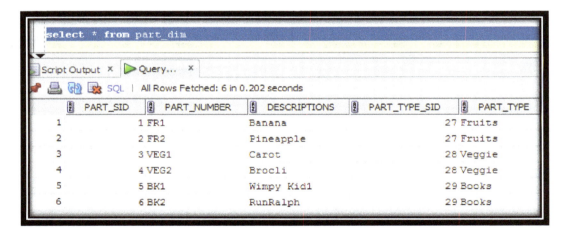

11 ELT using Joins

11.1 Data Set

11.1.1 Source

As part of this ELT, we are going to move below source data to target. During the ELT process, we are going to do a Join to TARGET.REGIONS_DIM table and get the REGION_SID.

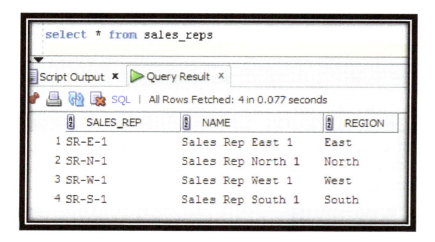

11.1.2 Target

The target table is empty now. After the ELT, all 4 records from the Source will be populated to the target table.

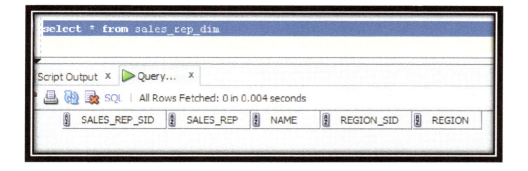

11.1.3 Expected Result

The target table is empty now. After the ELT, all 4 records from the Source will be populated to the target table.

11.2 Mapping

Create a new mapping by right clicking on 'Mapping' and then click on 'New Mapping'.

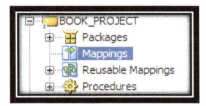

Click 'OK'

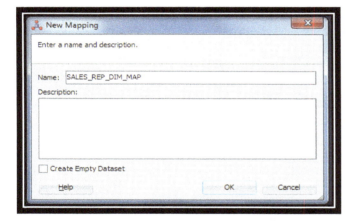

Click 'OK'

Drag and Drop SALES_REPS, REGIONS_DIM and SALE_REP_DIM as shown below:

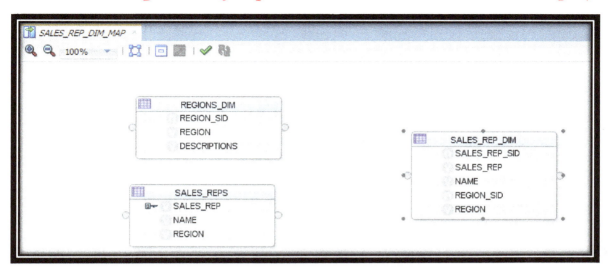

Click Join component

Drag and drop the 'JOIN'

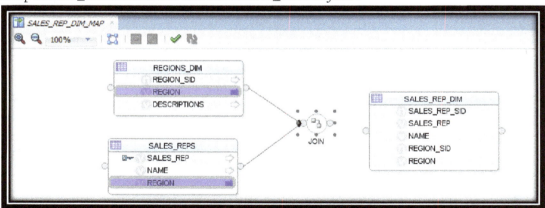

Drop SALES_REPS.REGION and REGIONS_DIM to JOIN

Click on 'JOIN'.

Go to the Property window.

Click on 'Condition'

Let us make the condition Outer join by checking Left Outer Join as shown below:

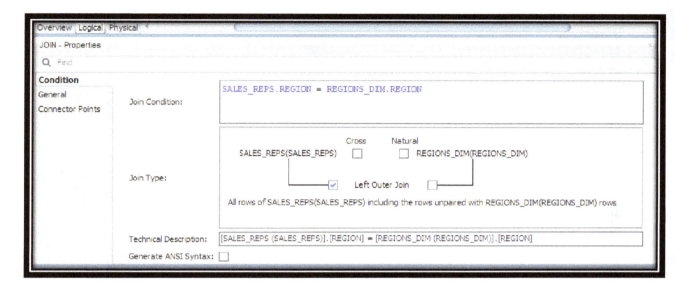

Drag and Drop source column to Target column as shown below:

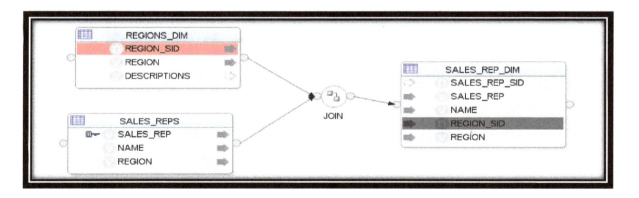

For SALE_REP_DIM.SALES_REP_SID column map sequence as shown below:

Click on 'SALES_REP_SID' column

Go to the property window

Go to expression editor

www.odijumpstart.com

Drag and drop SALES_REP_DIM_S sequence to the editor as shown below:

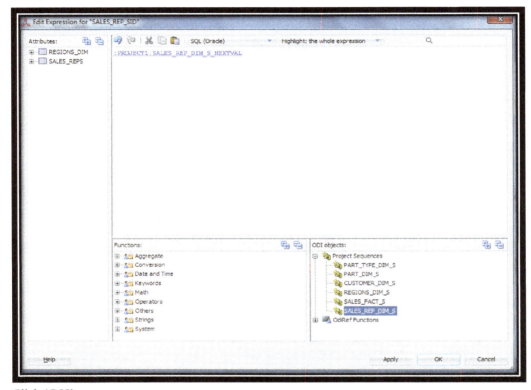

Click 'OK'

Click on 'JOIN'

Go to Property Window and click 'Connector Point'

You can review the INPUT and OUTPUT connectors.

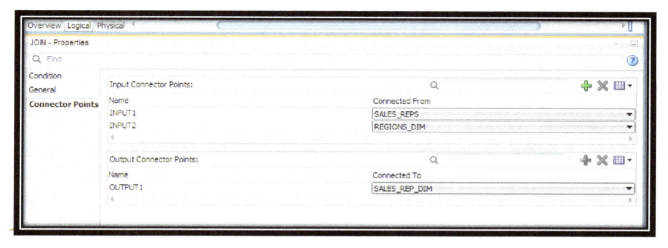

Save the ELT

Run the ELT

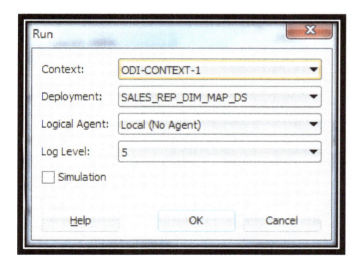

11.3 Actual Result

The result is as expected. All 4 records from the Source moved to Target. REGION_SID got populated using JOIN.

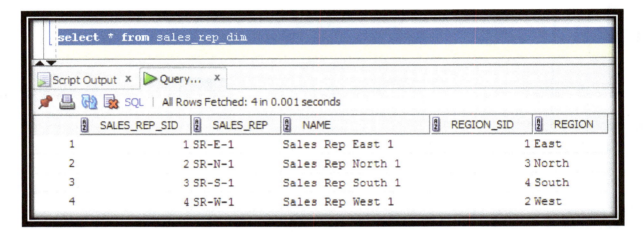

12 ELT using Union

12.1 Data Set

12.1.1 Source

As part of this ELT, we are going to move below source data to target. During the ELT process, we are going to use UNION to populate target table.

In order to use UNION component, we are going to divide the Source table into tables using Filter condition.

12.1.2 Target

The target table is empty now. After the ELT, all 4 records from the Source will be populated to the target table.

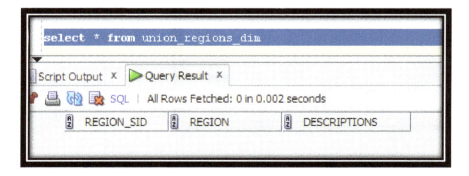

12.1.3   Expected Result

The target table is empty now. After the ELT, all 4 records from the Source will be populated to the target table.

12.2 Mapping

Create a new mapping by right clicking on 'Mapping' and then click on 'New Mapping'

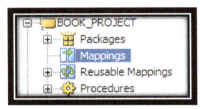

Click 'OK'

Click 'OK'

Drag and drop Source table 2 times since we are going to divide the table into 2.

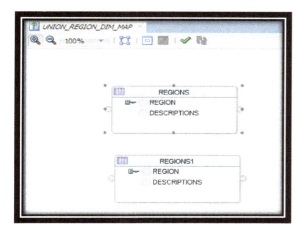

Let us divide the Source table into 2 tables by using Filter condition.

Let us group 'East' and 'West' in Group 1.

Drag 'REGION' out and create a filter as shown below:

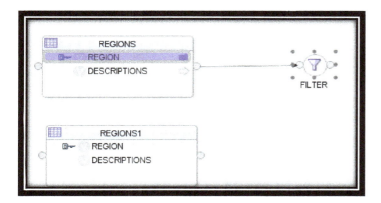

Click on 'FILTER' and add "where" condition as shown below:

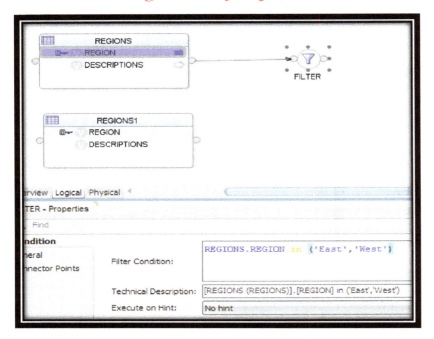

Let us group 'North' and 'South' in Group 2.

Drag 'REGION' from 'REGIONS1' to create a FILTER as shown below:

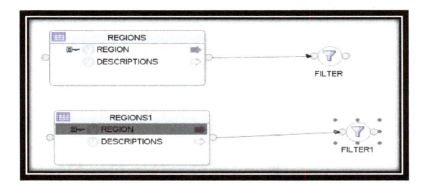

Click on 'FILTER1' and add "where" clause as shown below:

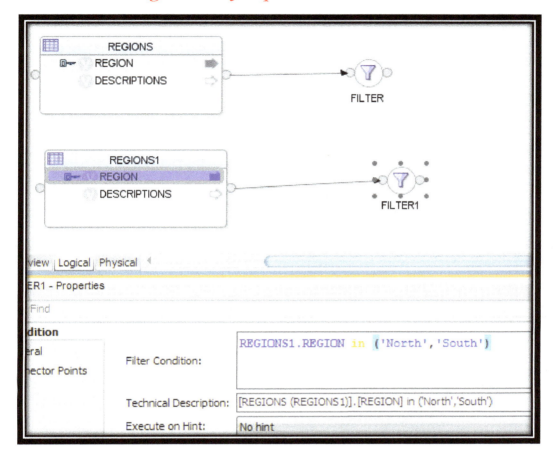

Now we created 2 data sources to capture all records from the source.

Let us use UNION to combine data from both and create a Target table.

Drag and Drop 'SET' component as shown below:

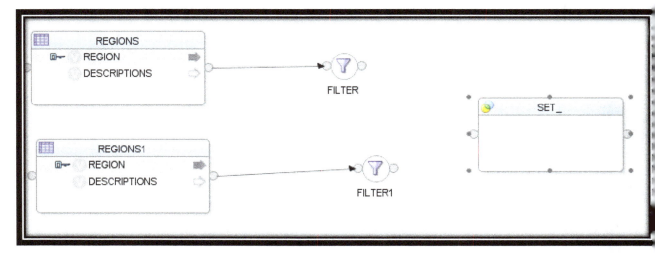

Drag and Drop the end connector from FILTER to SET.

You get the below Attribute Matching window:

Review and click OK.

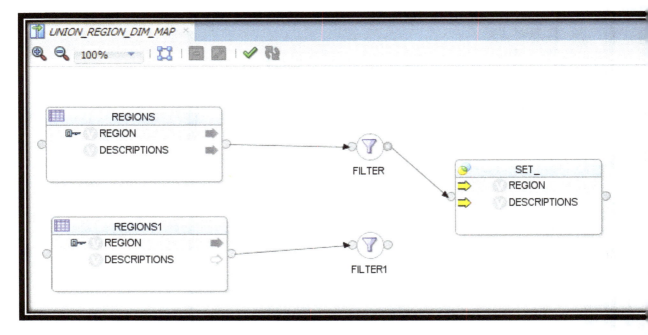

Drag and Drop Output connector from FILTER1 to SET.

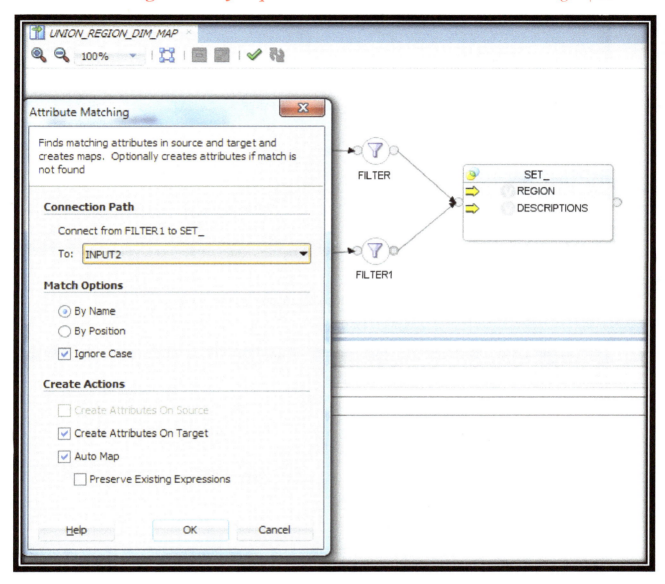

Review and click 'OK'

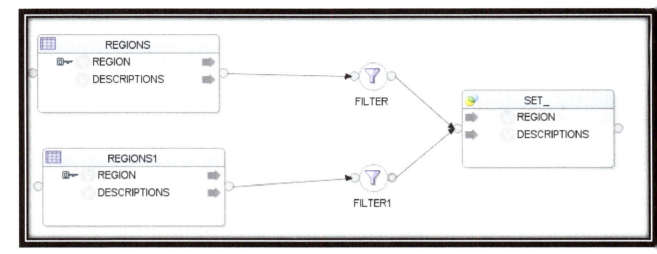

Drag and drop UNION_REGIONS_DIM table to the mapping as shown below:

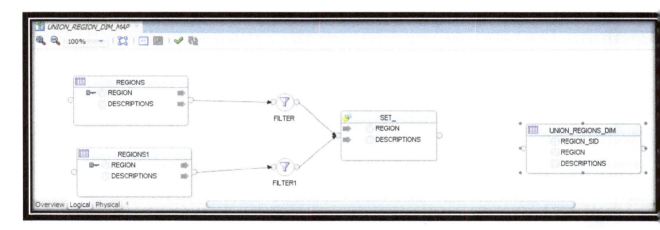

Map REGION and DESCRIPTIONS from SET to Target.

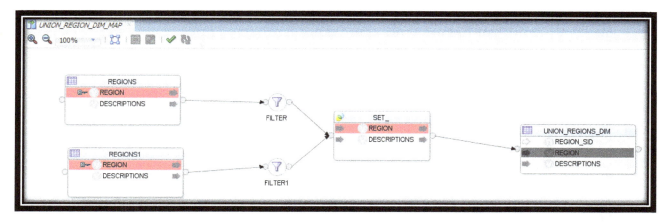

Assign Sequence to 'REGION_SID' as shown below:

Check 'Key'

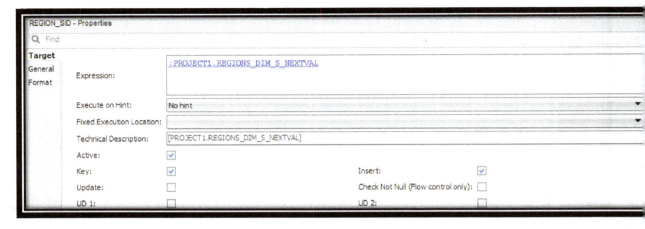

Click on 'SET_' and go to property window. Click on Operators as shown below:

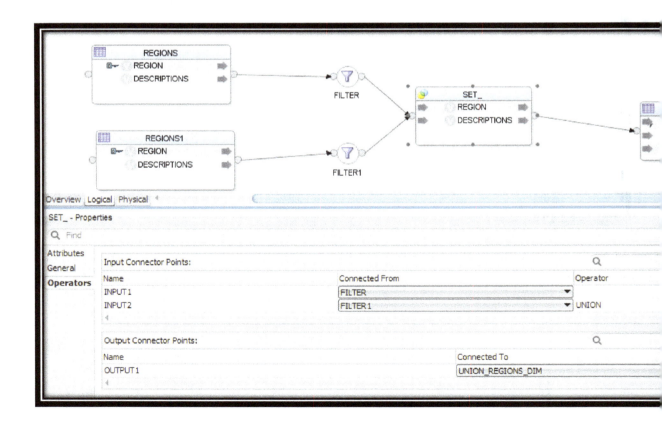

Review the INPUT and OUTPUT

Let us check the Physical

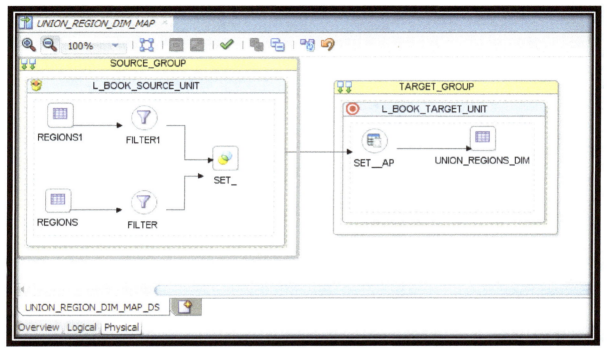

Click on 'SET_AP' and ensure that Loading Knowledge Module is 'LKM SQL to Oracle'

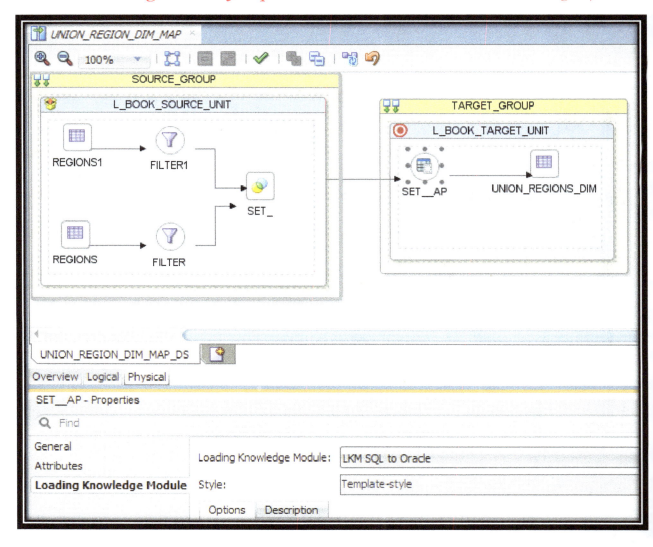

Click on 'UNION_REGIONS_DIM'

Pick 'IKM SQL Control Append' for Integration Knowledge Module'

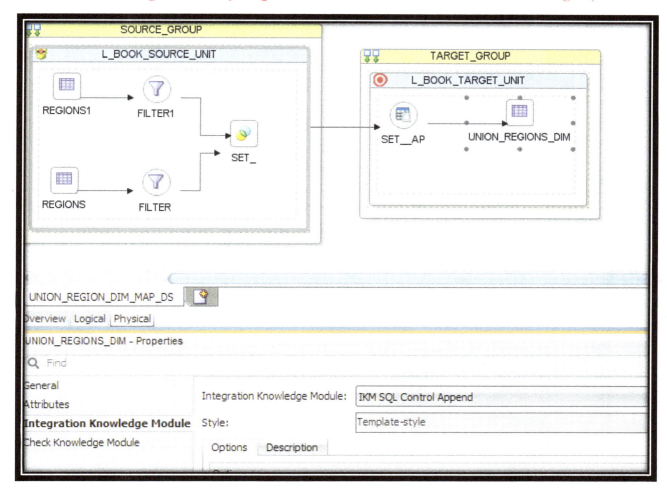

Pick 'CKM Oracle' for Check Knowledge Module

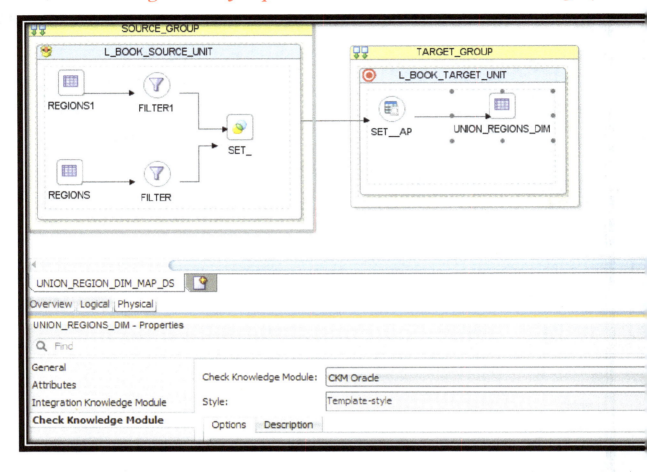

Save ELT

Run ELT

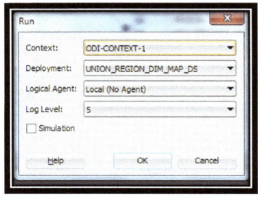

12.3 Actual Result

The result is as expected. All 4 records from the Source moved to Target. This result shows us how to use FILTER and UNION.

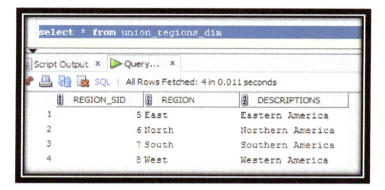

13 Flat File To Table ELT

As part of this example, you will learn how to upload a CSV file. In this example, you are going to learn how to configure, format and load. The upload file contains String, Number and Date. This will cover most of the upload requirements.

13.1 Data Set

13.1.1   Source

Below file will be uploaded into a table called FILE_UPLODE_TABLE

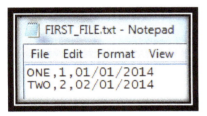

Save it to the D:

13.1.2   Expected Result

The FILE_UPLOAD_TABLE is empty now. After the ELT, the table will be populated with data from the file.

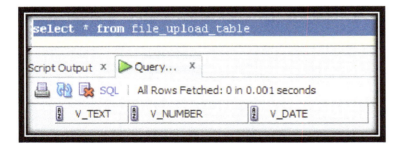

13.2 File Directory Setup

In this example, I use my local desktop as a file directory. You need to change file directory based on your needs.

13.3 Physical Connection

Go to Topology -> Physical Architecture -> Technologies -> File

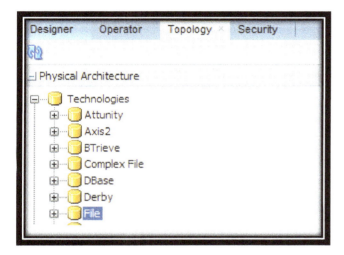

Right click on 'File'
Pick 'New Data Server'

Define the connection. Use user name and password.

Go to 'JDBC' section

For JDBC connection.

Pick ODI File JDBC Driver.

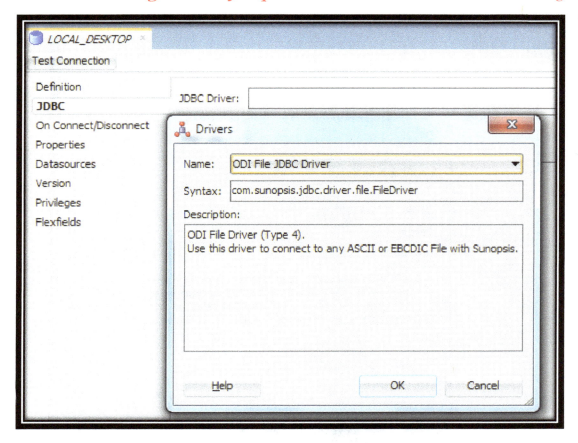

Assign JDBC URL as shown below:

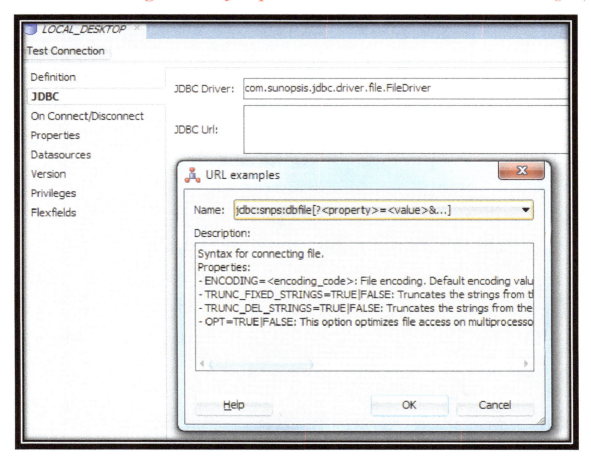

After the above 2 steps, the screen will look like as shown below:

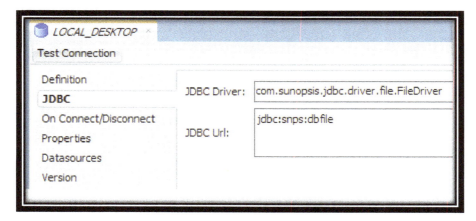

Test the connection

Click on 'Test Connection'

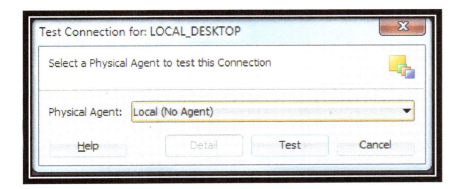

Click 'Test'

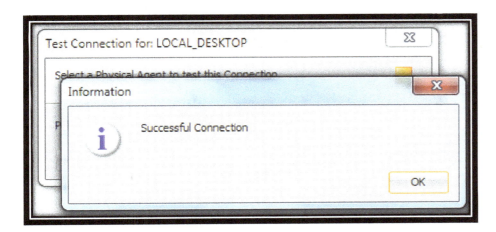

Click 'OK'

The connection tested successfully. Now we are done with connecting to the desktop.

Let us look at steps to define the Directory.

Go to 'Topology -> Physical Architecture -> Technologies -> File -> LOCAL_DESKTOP'

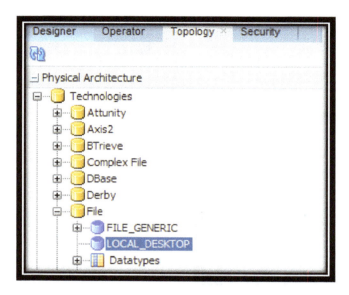

Right click
Pick 'New Physical Schema'
Set the directory to D:\ as shown below:

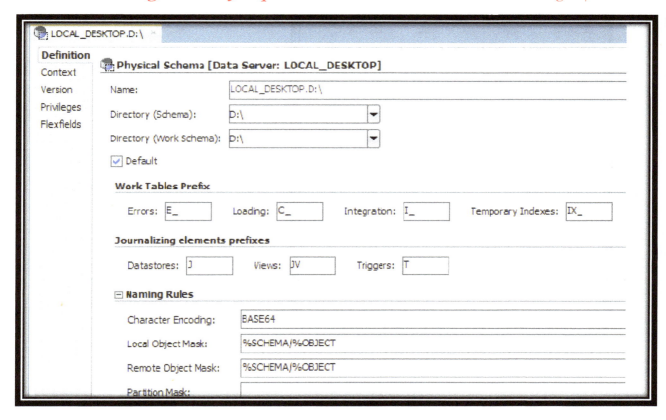

Save

You get the following warning message. Click 'OK'. We will attach logical schema later.

The Physical Architecture will look like as shown below:

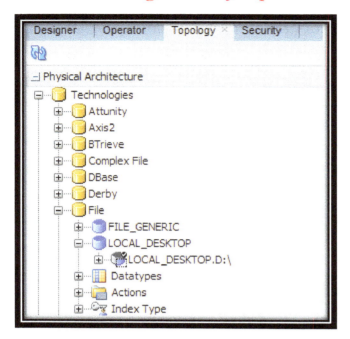

13.4 Logical Connection

Go to Topology -> Logical Architecture -> Technologies -> File

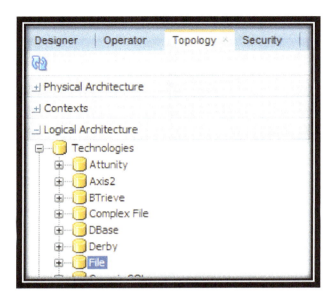

Right click on 'File'
Pick 'New Logical Schema'
Now associate logical schema to physical schema.
Define the logical schema as follows:

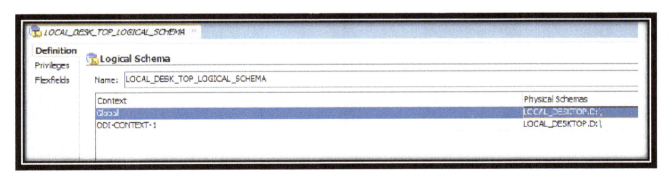

Save the schema

13.5 Model

Go to Designer - > Models

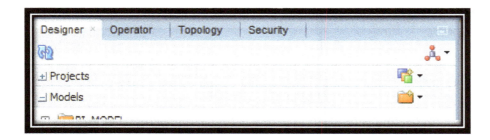

Click on

Pick 'New Model Folder'

Create model folder as shown below:

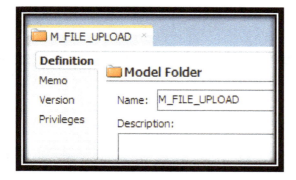

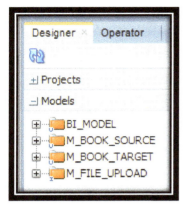

Click on

Right Click

Pick 'New Model'

Define a Model as shown below:

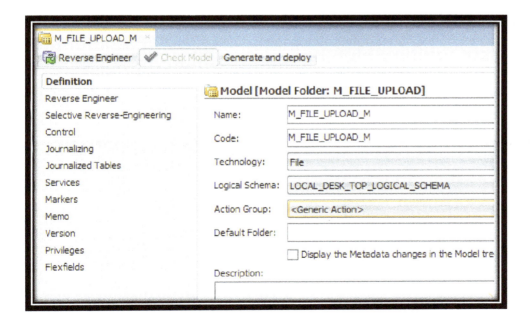

Designer will look like as shown below:

13.6 File Format

Click on 'M_FILE_UPLOAD_M'

Right click
Pick 'New Datastore'
Define a data store as shown below:

In this example, we are trying to load Comma separated file.

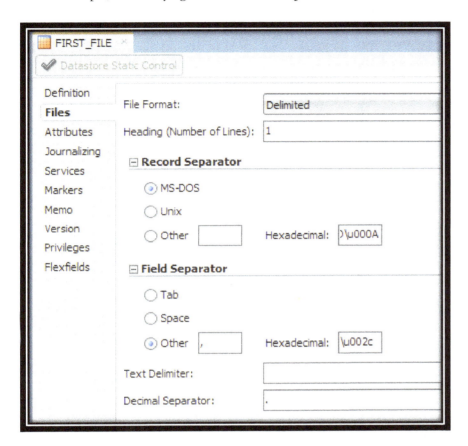

Click on Attributes.

We are going to define the fields in the file.

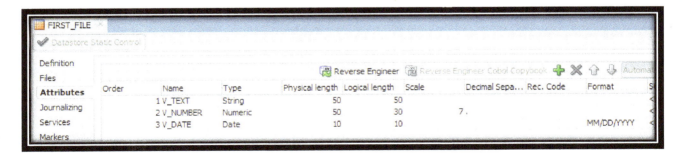

Save

The designer will look like as shown below:

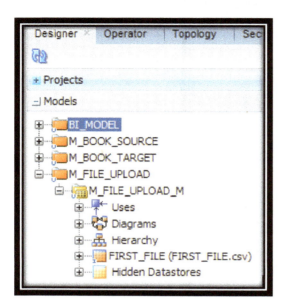

13.7 Create Table

Create table file_upload_table (v_text varchar2(50), v_number number(30,7), v_date date)

Import the table into Model

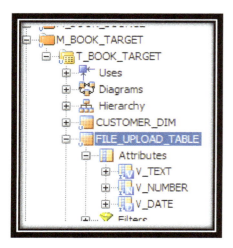

13.7.1.1 Prepare the file

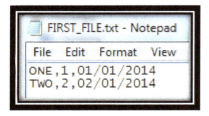

Save it to the D:

13.8 Mapping

Go to 'Designer -> Mappings

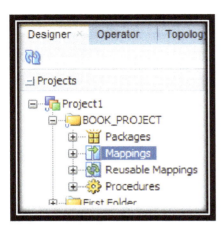

Right click on 'Mapping'

Click 'OK'

Drag and drop File and Table

Map corresponding fields.

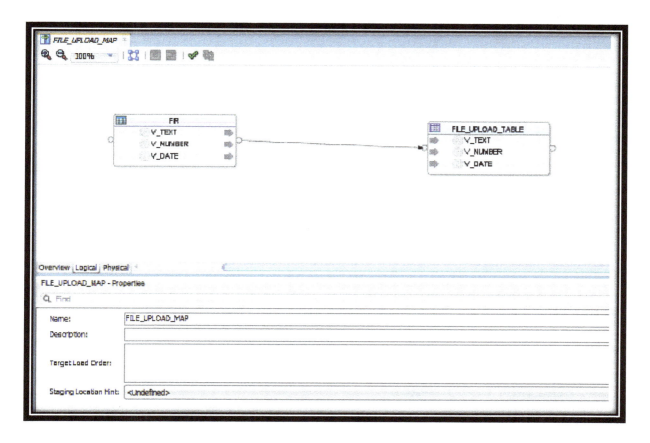

Click on 'Physical' to check the Physical diagram.

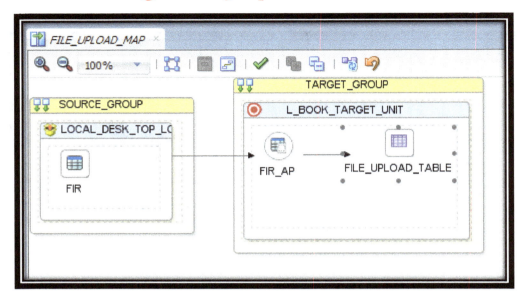

Click on 'FILE_UPLOAD_TABLE' and check 'Integration Knowledge Module'

In this case there is no need to change.

Click on 'FIR_AP' and check the Loading Knowledge Module.

Set NLS_DATE_LANGUAGE to MM/DD/YYYY

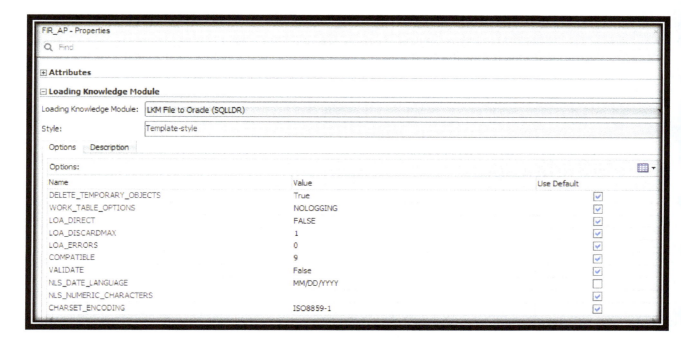

NOTE: Before running make sure to check your tnsnames.org file setup steps.

Run

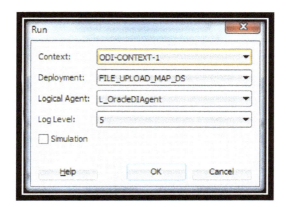

Click OK

13.9 tnsnames.ora setup

In this example we are using SQL loader knowledge module to load data from the file. Oracle recommends using SQL loader for large data set. The database is running on localhost. Depending on your setup, you may need to use different tnsnames entry.

13.9.1.1 tns file

```
localhost =
 (DESCRIPTION =
  (ADDRESS = (PROTOCOL = TCP)(HOST = localhost)(PORT = 1521))
  (CONNECT_DATA =
   (SERVER = DEDICATED)
   (SERVICE_NAME = orcl)
  )
 )
```

13.10 Actual Result

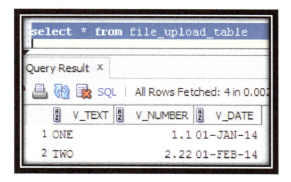

14 Using Markers

14.1 Generate Multiple Scenarios using Markers

For ODI Package creation, please refer to the ODI Packages section in this book.

In this example we are going to group more than one ODI Packages using marker and regenerate the Packages.

Below are the 2 Packages we are going to use in this example:

Right Click on 'PART_DIM_MAP_PKG'

Add Marker -> Smiley -> Smiley1

You can see 'Similey1' marked against 'PART_DIM_MAP_PKG'

Repeat the same for 'PART_TYPE_DIM_MAP_PKG'

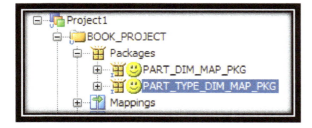

Now let us generate both the Packages using Marker

Right Click on BOOK_PROJECT and pick 'Generate All Scenarios ..'

You will get the below as shown window:

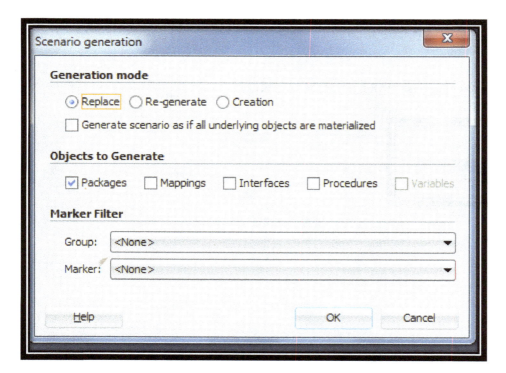

Pick 'Re-Generate'
Pick 'Packages'
Pick 'Group'
Pick 'Marker'

As shown below:

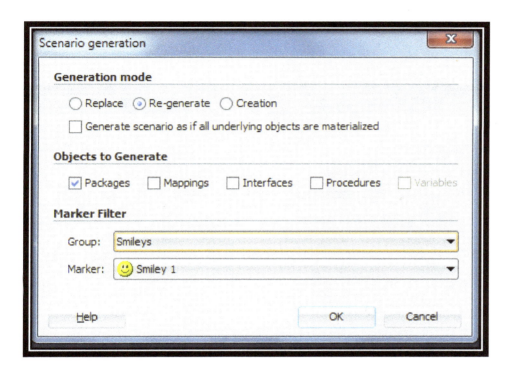

Click 'OK' to re-generate.

15 ODI 12c New Features - Reusable Mappings

The advantage of reusable mapping is that you create it once and use it as many times as you want.

In this example, let us create a mapping to convert a text to upper case based on an ID, and use it on a regular mapping.

15.1 Data Set

15.1.1 Source

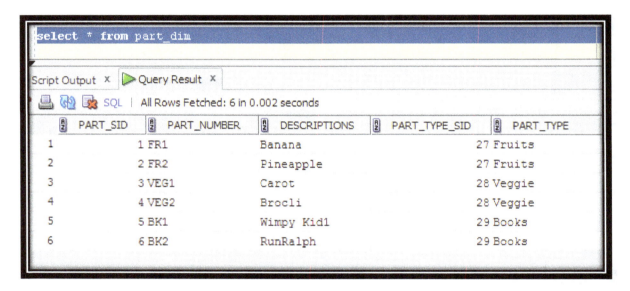

15.1.2 Expected Result

We are going to use 'Reusable Mapping' to convert the Descriptions to Upper case.
All Descriptions value in the PART_DIM table will be converted to Upper case.

15.2 Mapping

Go to Designer.

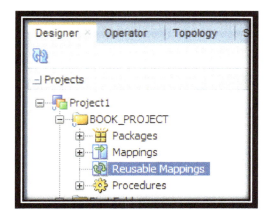

Right click on 'Reusable mappings'
Pick 'Create New Reusable mappings'

Clicking 'OK' will create a new reusable mapping as shown below:

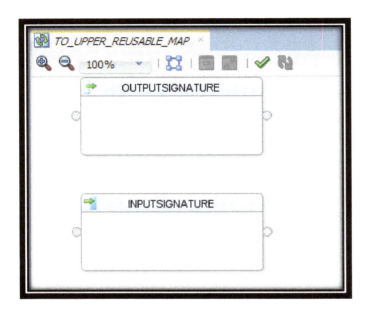

Let us create 2 new attributes to 'INPUTSIGNATURE'.
Click on 'INPUTSIGNATURE'
Go to 'Property' Window

Add 2 new attributes by clicking on '+' sign.

ID - Number (30)
INPUT_VALUE - Varchar2 (2000)

Let us create 2 new attributes to 'OUTPUTSIGNATURE'.
Click on 'OUTPUTSIGNATURE'
Go to 'Property' Window
Add 2 new attributes by clicking on '+' sign.
ID - Number (30)
OUTPUT_UPPER_VALUE - Varchar2 (2000)

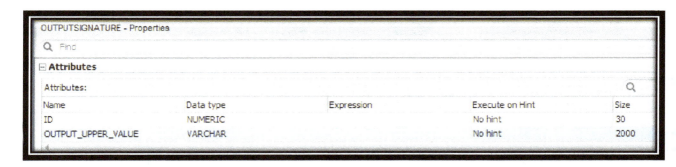

Let us map input and output.
Drag and Drop ID and INPUT_VALUE to 'OUTPUTSIGNATURE'.

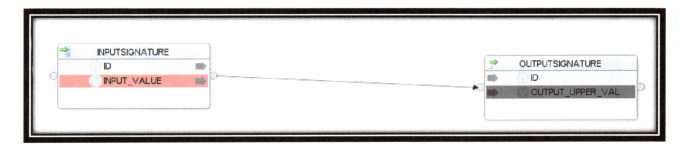

Click on 'OUTPUT_UPPER_VALUE' and go to Property.

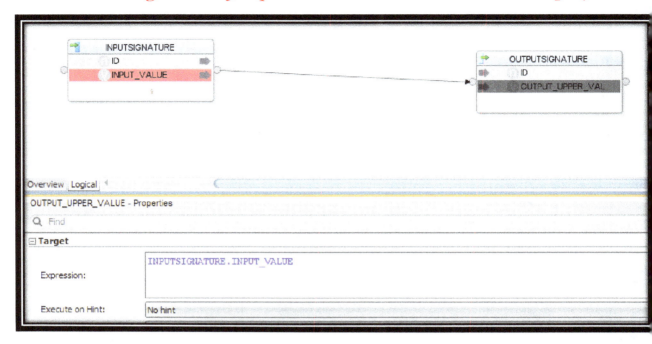

As you can see, it is mapped to INPUTSIGNATURE.INPUT_VALUE

Let us add UPPER to it in order to convert the value to Upper.

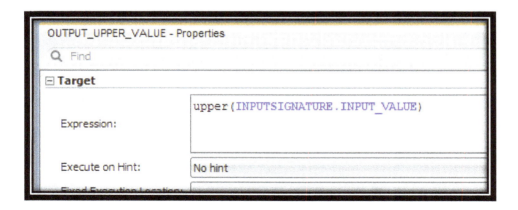

Now the 'Reusable Mapping' is ready for usage.

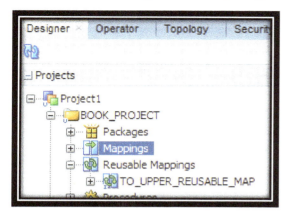

Let us create a new mapping and use the Upper case reusable mapping inside.

Go to 'Designer'
Go to 'Mapping'
Right click
Pick 'New Mapping'

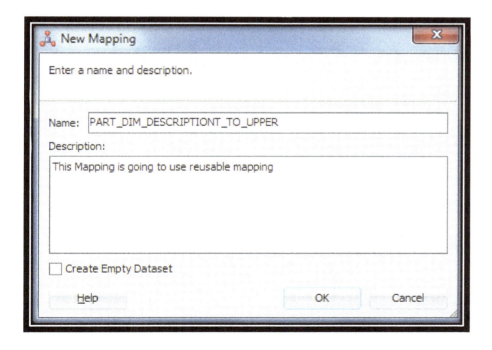

You get an empty mapping.

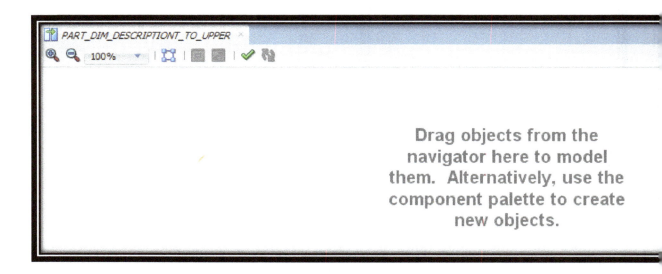

Drag and Drop PART_DIM from Model to the mapping two times.

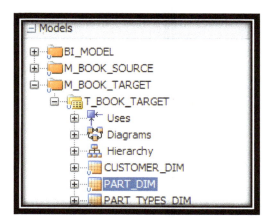

In this case both source and target are the same.

Let us drag and drop 'Reusable Mapping'

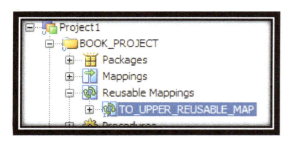

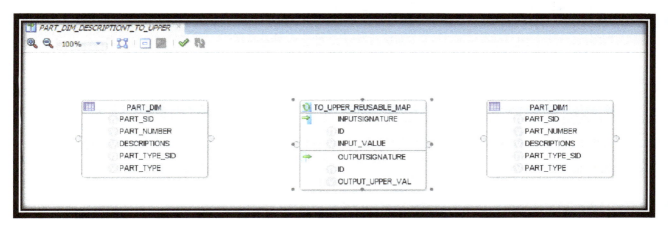

Map the PART_SID and DESCRIPTION to Reusable mapping INPUT side

Click on 'TO_UPPER_REUSABLE_MAP' to check the Property

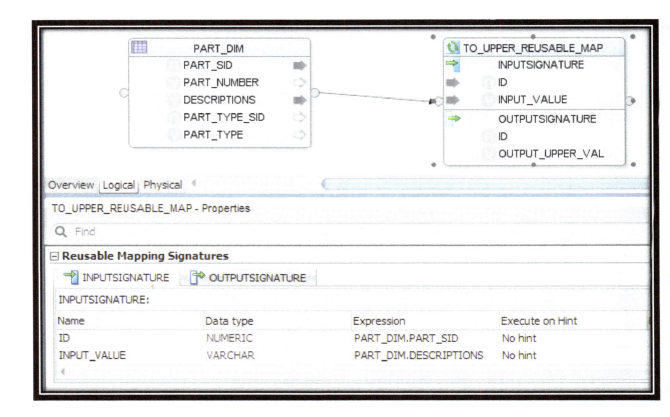

Map the OUTPUTSIGNATURE fields to PART_DIM (Target)
Click on 'PART_DIM' Target to check the Property

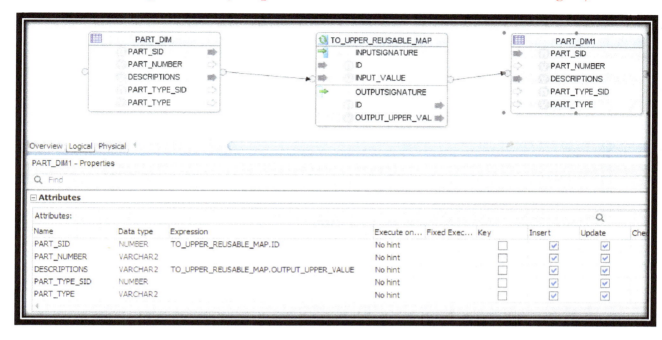

Change the PART_DIM (Target) name for easy identification

Go to Target -> Integration Type
Pick 'Incremental Update'.
In this example we are going to update existing records.

Define a key at the 'Target'
Go to 'PART_DIM_TARGET' and click on 'PART_SID'

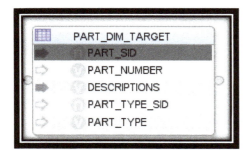

Check 'Key'

Uncheck 'Update'

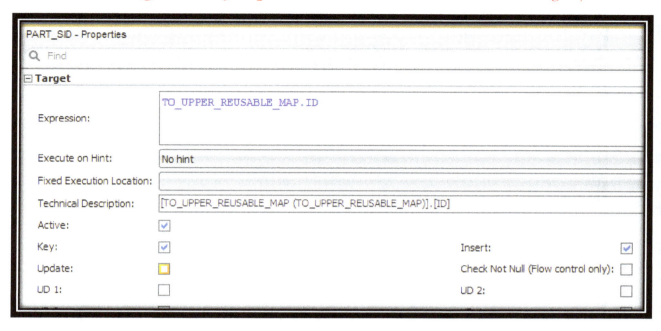

Click on 'Physical'

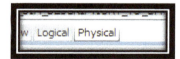

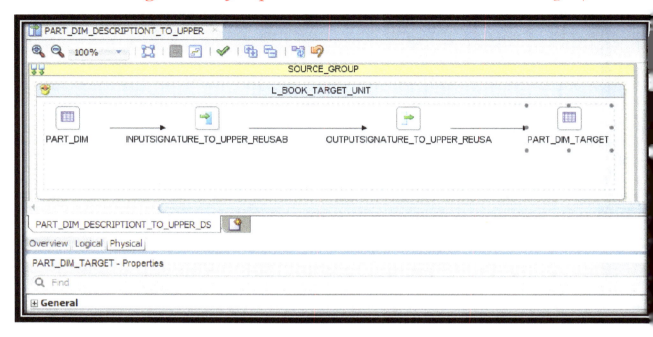

Click on 'PART_DIM_TARGET'

Make the 'Integration knowledge Module' to IKM Oracle Incremental Update.

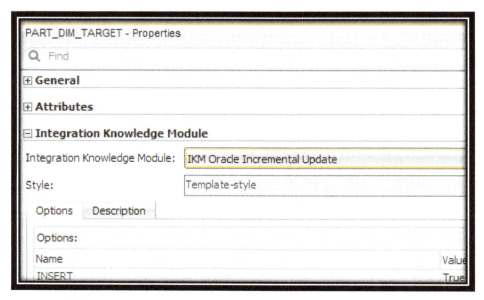

Run the mapping.

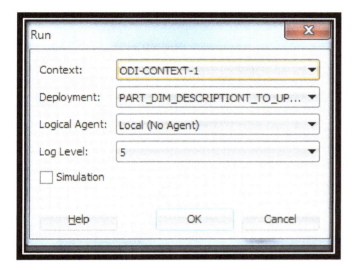

15.3 Actual Result

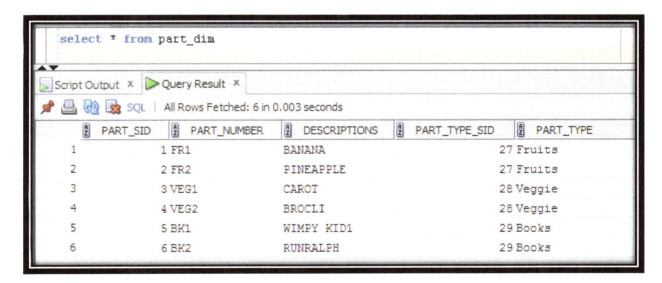

16 ODI 12c New Features - SPLIT (One Source Table to Multiple Target Tables)

16.1 Data Set

16.1.1 Source

As part of this ELT, we are going to move below source data to target. During the ELT process, we are going to use SPLIT to populate the target table.

We are going to split 4 records into 4 Target tables.

16.1.2 Target

The target table is empty now. After the ELT, all 4 records from the Source will be populated to the target table.

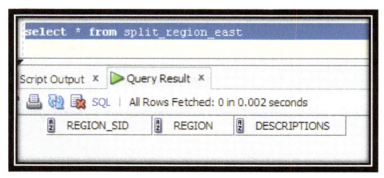

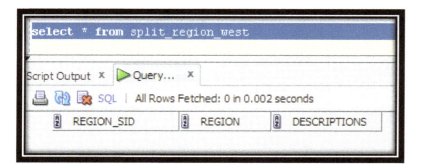

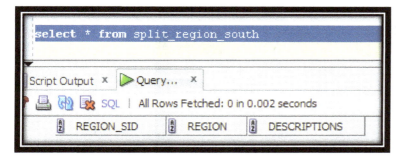

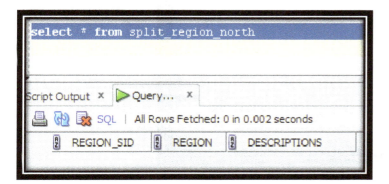

16.1.3   Expected Result

The target tables are empty now. After the ELT, all 4 records from the Source will be populated to the target table; one records each.

16.2 Mapping

Create a new mapping by right clicking on 'Mapping' and then click on 'New Mapping'

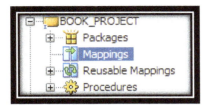

Click 'OK'

Click 'OK'

Drag REGIONS_DIM as shown below:

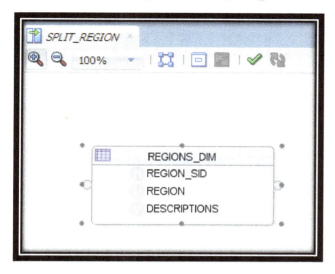

Drag and drop SPLIT component

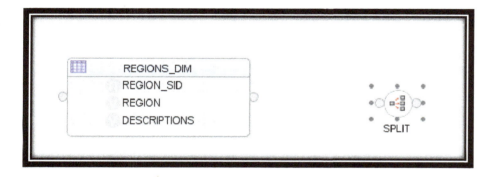

Drop 'REGION' into SPLIT

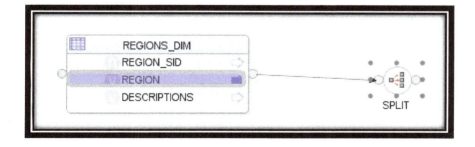

Drag and Drop all 4 Target tables

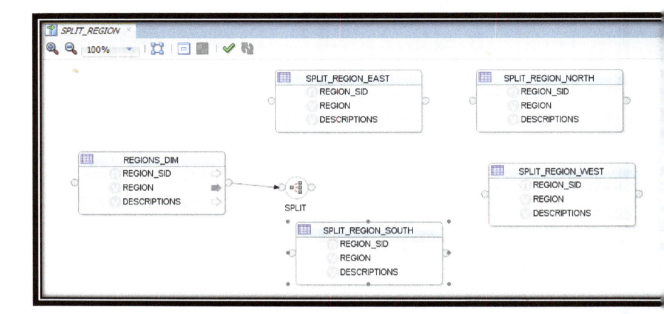

Drag and drop SPLIT output connector to SPLIT_REGION_SOUTH

Attribute Matching window below will open.

Review and click OK.

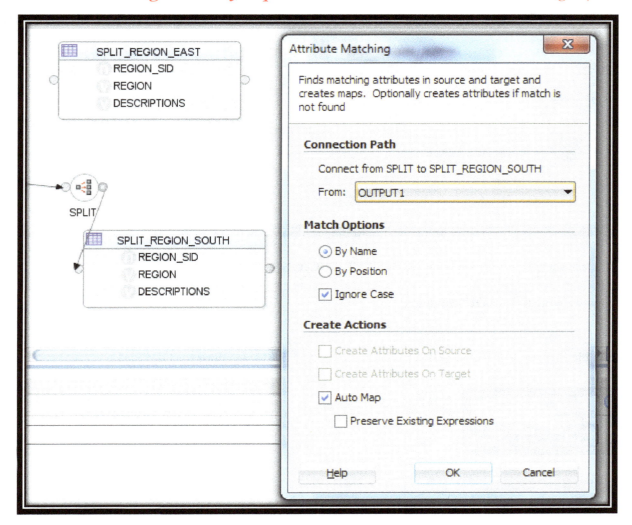

Click on 'SPLIT' and go to Property window.

Go to Split Conditions

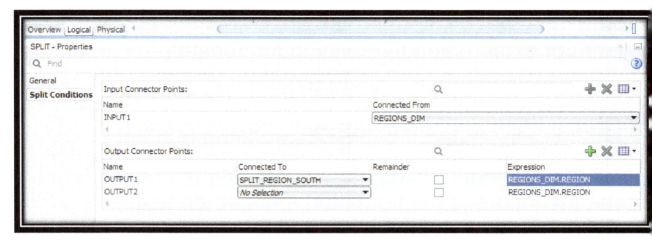

You can see OUTPUT1 is connected to SPLIT_REGION_SOUTH

Now we write the "where" condition.

Double click on 'REGIONS_DIM.REGION' to go to Expression editor for OUTPUT1

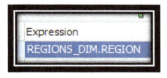

Add "where" condition.

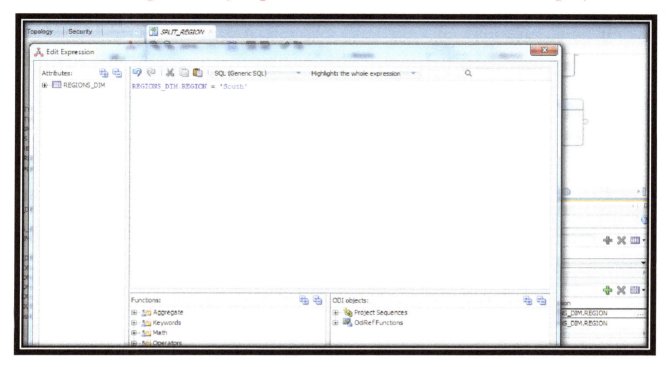

Repeat the same for North.

By Default SPLIT created 2 Split conditions. Add 2 more Split conditions by adding more Output
Connector Points.

After adding 2 more OUTPUT connectors, Property window will look like as shown below:

Now Drag SPLIT output connector to East and North.

Add Expression

Add adding all Expressions. Property window will look like as shown below:

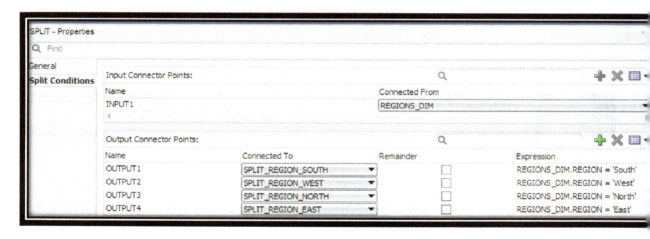

Mapping will look like as shown below:

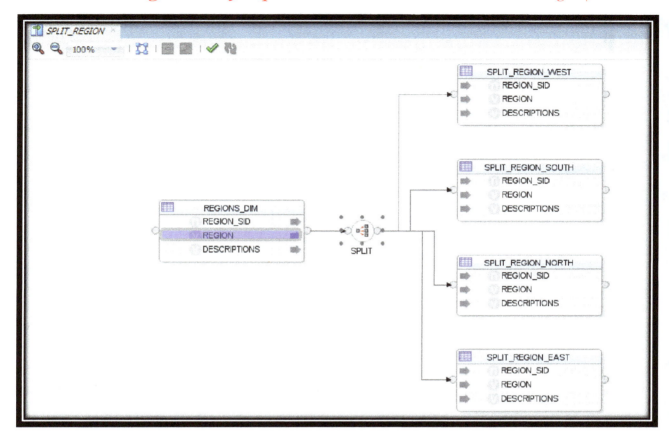

Assign key, click SPLIT_REGION_WEST and go to Property window.
Check Key and Uncheck Update

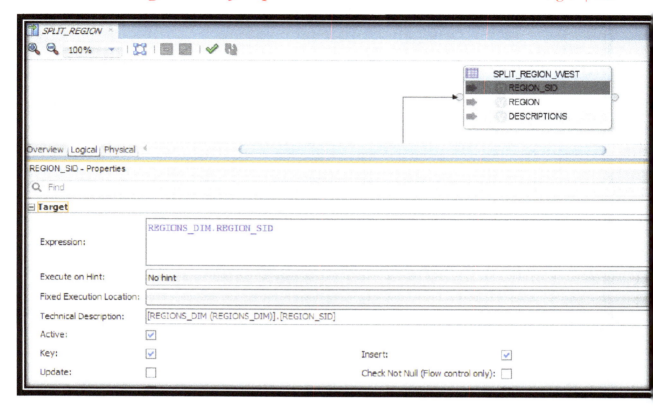

Repeat the same for South, East, and North.

Let us look at Physical

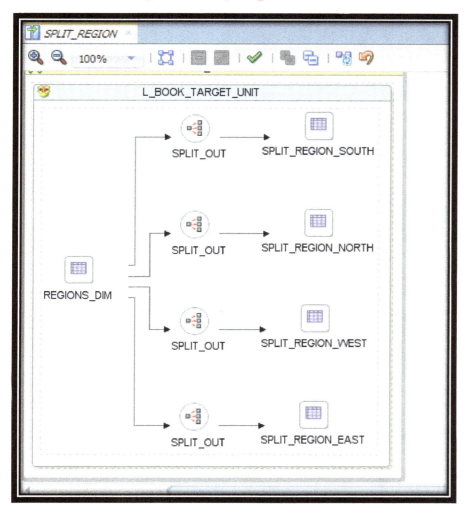

Select SPLIT_REGION_SOUTH and pick IKM SQL Control Append as Integration Knowledge Module

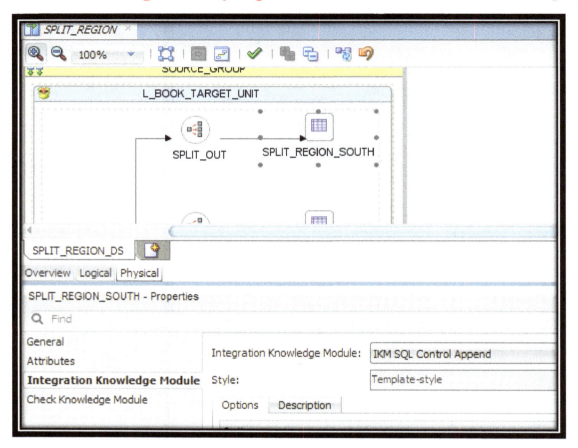

Repeat the same for North, East and West

Save the ELT

Run the ELT

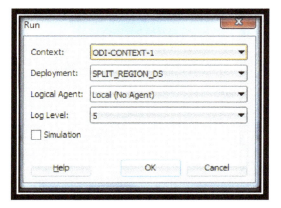

16.3 Actual Result

The result is as expected, All 4 records from the Source moved to 4 Target tables. This result shows us how to use SPLIT.

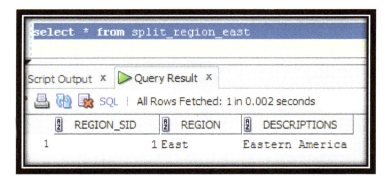

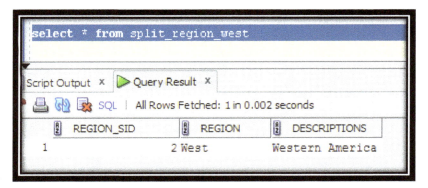

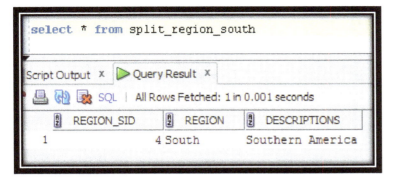

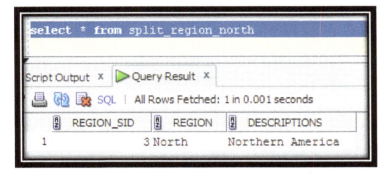

17 ODI Packages

17.1 Package Creation

Go to Designer -> Project -> Packages

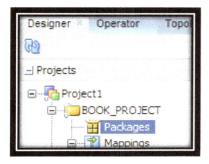

Right Click and create new Package

Click 'OK'

You will get the 'Diagram' window as shown below:

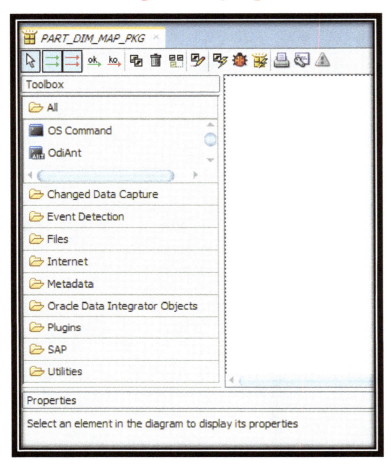

Drag and drop PART_DIM_MAP into the Diagram window

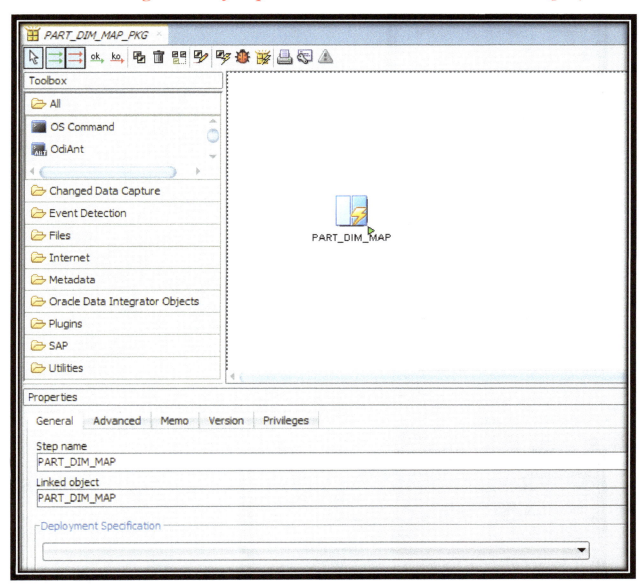

Save

17.2 Scenario Creation

Go to Packages

Expand PART_DIM_MAP_PKG

Right click on PART_DIM_MAP_PKG and pick a popup window will open

Select 'Generate Scenario'
OK to create Scenario

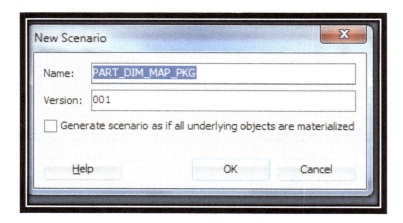

After Scenario creation

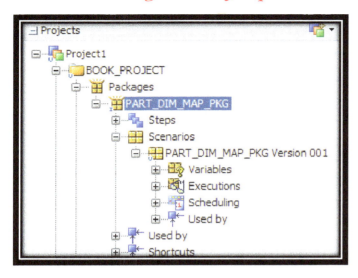

Now the scenario can be executed.

18 ODI Procedures

In this example let us look at writing a DML script or PL/SQL block in the ODI Procedure

18.1 Data Set

18.1.1 Source

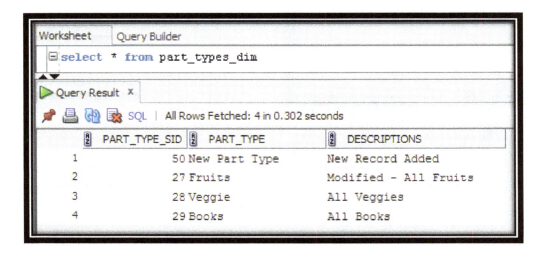

18.1.2 Expected Result

As part of this Procedure we are going to add '-TEST-' to the DESCRIPTIONS.

18.2 ODI Procedure Creation

Go to 'Designer'
Click on Procedure

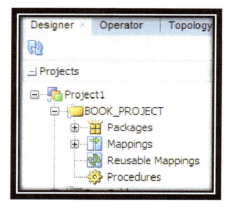

Right Click on 'Procedures' and pick 'New Procedure'
Define the Procedure

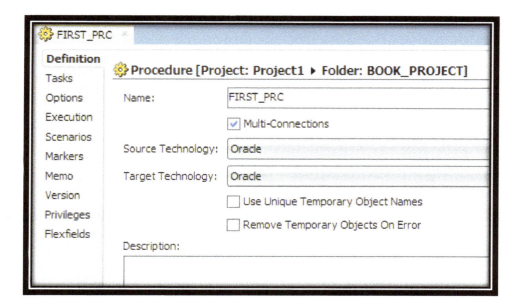

Enter Name -> FIRST_PRC
Check Multi-Connections
Source Technology -> Oracle
Target Technology -> Oracle
Click on 'Task'

Add a New Task by clicking add icon.

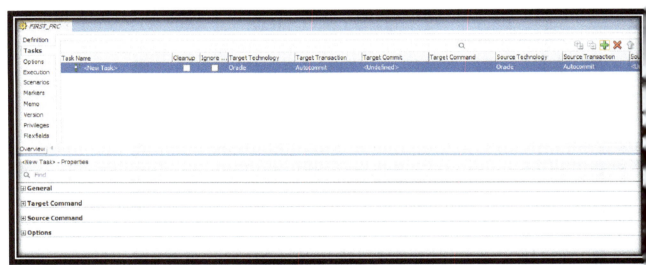

Go to 'Property'
Expand 'Target Command'

Set Schema;

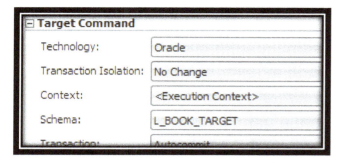

Go to 'Command'

Go to 'Command Advance Editor'

Enter an 'UPDATE STATEMENT'

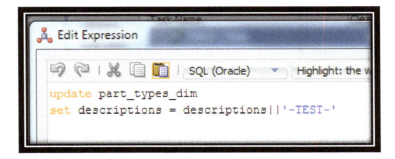

Click 'OK'

> **NOTE**: The command can be a PL/SQL block with DECLARE, BEGIN and END.
> Run the Procedure

18.3 Actual Result

As you can see below, DESCRIPTIONS appended with '-TEST-'

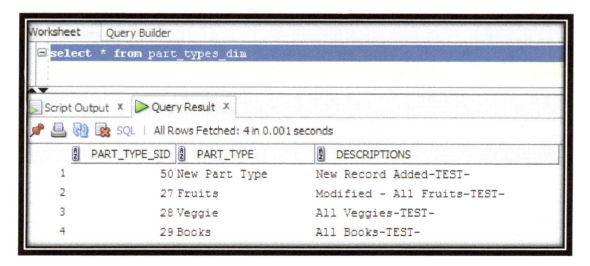

19 ODI Variables

You can define variables and it can be populated using Select statements. These variables can be used in Packages as runtime variables.

Go to 'Designer'
Right Click on 'Variables'

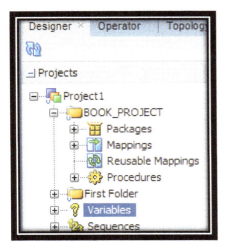

Pick 'New Variable'
Define Variable

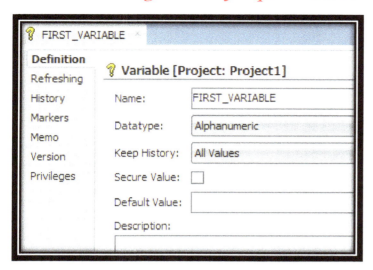

Name: FIRST_VARIABLE
Data Type: Alphanumeric
Keep History: All Values

Go to 'Refreshing'
Select Schema

Write a SQL code using ODI Functions as shown below:

Save
Click Refresh button to run the SQL

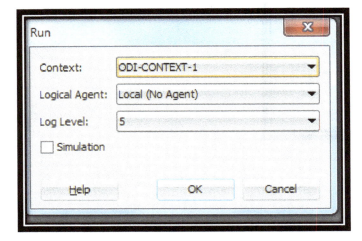

Check the 'Operator' for successful completion
Click on the 'History' tab to see the value

It returns the number of records, satisfies the SQL statement. New variables created and it is available in the ODI. They can be used in Mapping, Packages.

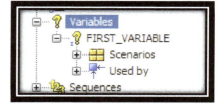

20 Code Migration

In this example, it is assumed that you have 3 independent environments called Development, UAT and Production. ODI is installed on all 3 environments.

ODI provides a mechanism called Export/Import Objects from ODI. When doing an export you can pick one or more objects to export. The objects get exported in XML format.

ODI imports the Objects using the exported XML files.

Let us see how this is done.

In this example, you are going to see how to export multiple Objects.

Go to 'Designer' and click Export button.

Pick 'Export'

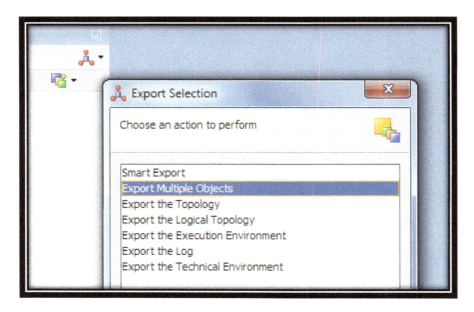

Pick 'Export Multiple Objects'

Click 'OK'

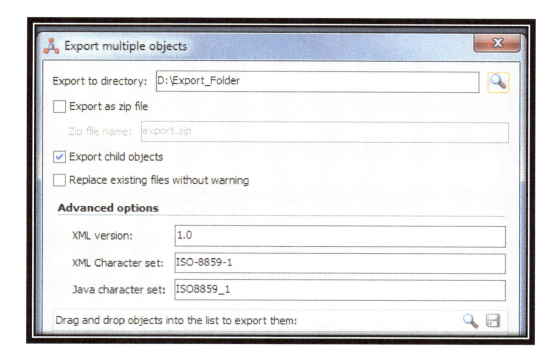

Select the 'Export to directory'

Make Export child objects checked.

Drag and Drop 2 mappings,

PARTY_TYPE_DIM_MAP

PARTY_TYPE_DIM_INCREMENTAL_MAP

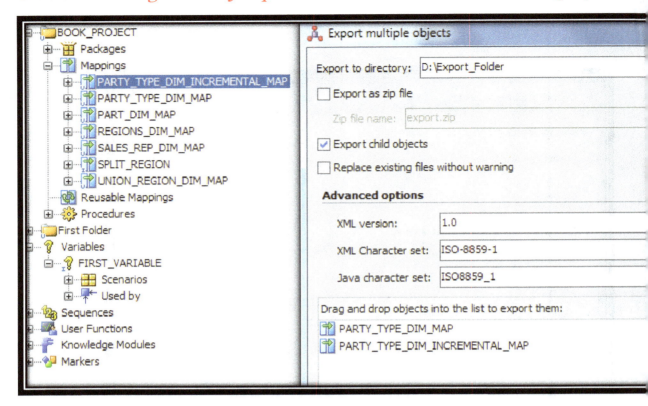

Click 'OK'

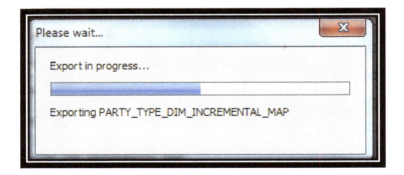

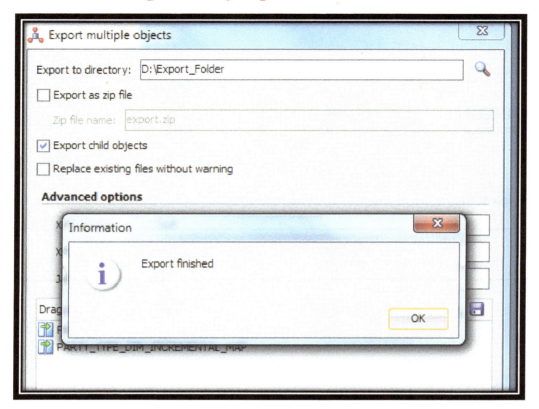

The check the XML file, go the Export folder.

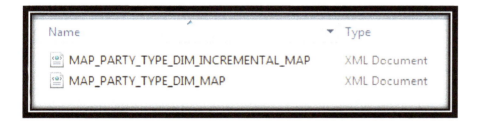

Import Objects
To Import Objects
Go Designer
Click on Project

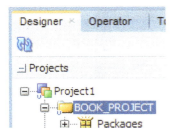

Right Click
Pick 'Import'
Pick appropriate object type.

NOTE: Import can be done at Package, Mapping, Variable etc.. levels
In case of Smart Export, Use Smart Import to Import it.

---

21 Load Planner

In this example, we will see how to create a load plan. Using Load plan, you can automate the execution of multiple scenarios in a specific sequence. During the load, you have the ability to run scenarios in a Serial or Parallel mode.

We are going to create a Plan with one Serial step and one Parallel step

Serial Step using two Package scenarios PART_DIM_MAP_PKG and PART_TYPE_DIM_MAP_PKG

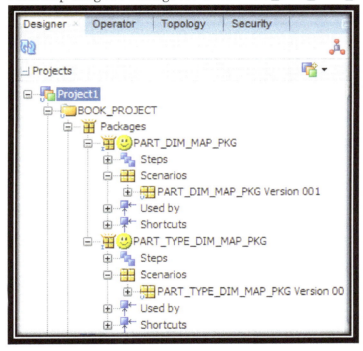

Serial Step using 2 mapping scenarios REGIONS_DIM_MAP and SALES_REP_DIM_MAP

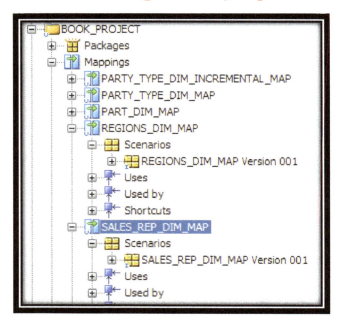

> **NOTE**: For the above 2 mappings, there is no scenario available at this time. You will
> Notice that once we add the mapping to the Load plan, the scenario will be automatically created. You can
> also create the scenario in advance for the mapping.

21.1 Plan Creation

Go to Designer -> Load Planner

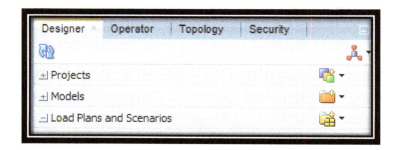

Click on

Pick 'New Load Plan and Scenario Folder'

Create MY_LOAD_PLAN Folder as shown below and save.

It will create a Load Plan folder as shown below:

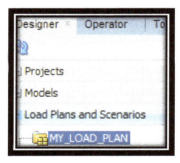

Right Click on 'MY_LOAD_PLAN'

Pick 'New Load Plan'

Define a new plan called 'First Load Plan'

Click on 'Steps'

By default 'root_step' gets created with 'Serial' step type.

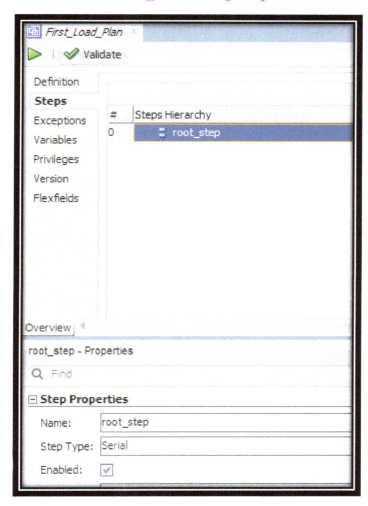

Add a Parallel step by clicking on the Plus sign. Pick 'Parallel Step'

This will create a Parallel step as shown below:

Change the name of the step to 'First Parallel Step'

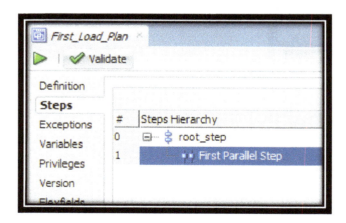

Now Drag and Drop, "PART_DIM_MAP_PKG Version 001" into the 'First Parallel Step'.

NOTE: You need to drop it on top of 'First Parallel Step'

Now Drag and Drop, "PART_TYPE_DIM_MAP_PKG Version 001" into the 'First **Parallel Step**'.

NOTE: You need to drop it on top of 'First Parallel Step'

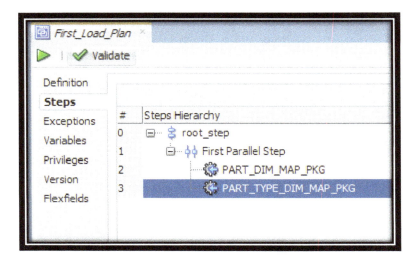

Now let us create a serial step group using the mapping.

Click on 'root_step'

Add a Serial step by clicking on the Plus sign. Pick 'Serial Step'

This will create a Serial step as shown below:

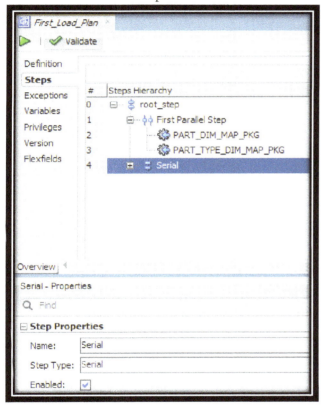

Change the name to 'First Serial Step'

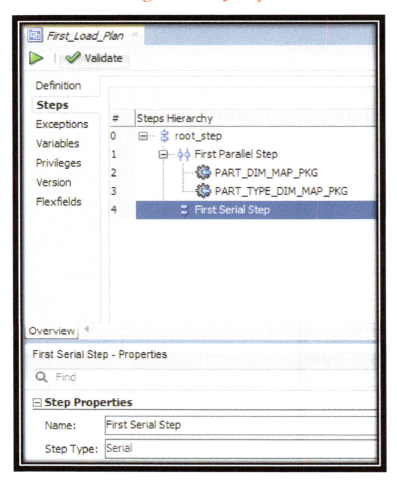

Now let us add two mappings

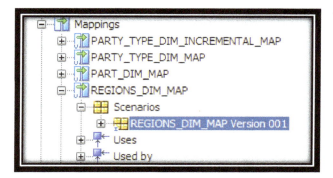

Drag and Drop 'REGIONS_DIM_MAP' mapping into 'First Serial Step'

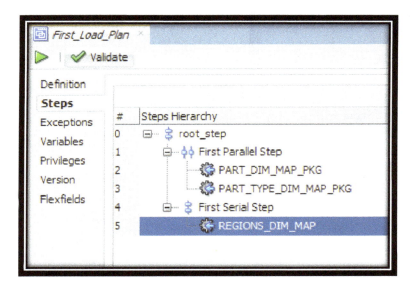

Drag and Drop 'SALES_REP_DIM_MAP' mapping into 'First Serial Step'

Now we created one Parallel step and one Serial step.

Save the Plan. You will notice 'First_Load_Plan' load plan added to 'MY_LOAD_PLAN' folder.

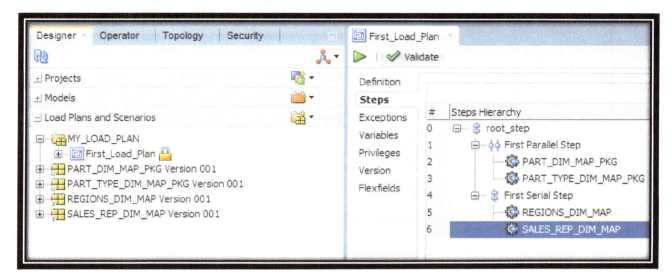

21.2 Plan Execution

Click on 'First Load Plan'

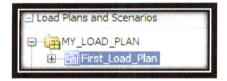

Execute the Plan

21.3 Plan Scheduling

Plan can be scheduled by multiple ways

Expand the 'First_Load_Plan'

Right Click on 'Scheduling'

Pick 'New Scheduling'

Pick 'Logical Agent'
Pick 'Context'

This plan will run Daily at 9:00 PM.

Load Plan Scheduling ODI_CONTEXT_1 /L_OracleDIAgent ×

Definition
Execution Cycle
Variables
Privileges
Version

Scheduling [Load Plan: First_Load_Plan]

Context: ODI-CONTEXT-1 ▼   Logical Agent: L_OracleDIAgent ▼

Log Level: 5 ▼

⊟ **Status**

⦿ Active
◯ Inactive
◯ Active for the period:

☐ Starting: Date: Jun 24, 2014 ▼   Time: 7:37:12 AM ⬍ 🗓
☐ Ending   Date: Jun 24, 2014 ▼   Time: 7:37:12 AM ⬍ 🗓
☐ Every day between: from: 7:37:12 AM ⬍   to: 7:37:12 AM ⬍
☐ Except these days of the month
☐ Except these days of the week: ☐ Monday ☐ Tuesday ☐ Wednesday ☐ Thursday
                                      ☐ Friday ☐ Saturday ☐ Sunday

⊟ **Execution**

◯ On startup   Time: 9:00:00 PM ⬍
◯ Simple
◯ Hourly
⦿ Daily
◯ Weekly
◯ Monthly (day of the month)
◯ Monthly (week day)
◯ Yearly

21.4 Plan Update Schedule

In order to run the plan on a daily basis, the above plan needs to be added to 'Agen Schedule'. Unless it gets added, plan will not be executed on a daily basis. To update schedule, follow steps below:

Go to 'Topology'

Go to 'Physical Architecture'

Click on Agents

Expand Agents

Right Click on 'OracleDIAgent'

Pick 'Update Schedule'

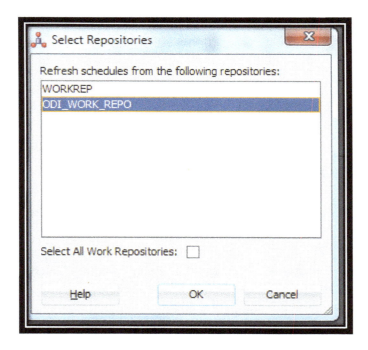

Pick a valid repositories
Press 'OK'

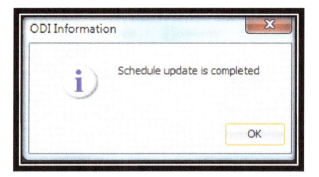

To verify the scheduler,

Go to 'Topology' and right click on 'OracleDIAgent'

Right click on 'OracleDIAgent' and pick 'View Schedule..'

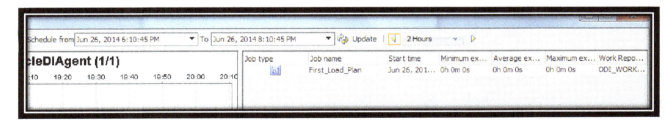

22 Appendix A - Database Objects Creation Scripts

Below are the table creation scripts for Source and Target schemas.

22.1 Source Schema

22.1.1 Table Creation

```
--------------------------------------------------------
-- DDL for Table CUSTOMERS
--------------------------------------------------------

 CREATE TABLE BOOK_SOURCE.CUSTOMERS
 (      CUSTOMER VARCHAR2(100),
        NAME VARCHAR2(500),
        REGION VARCHAR2(50)
 ) ;
--------------------------------------------------------
-- DDL for Table PART_TYPES
--------------------------------------------------------

 CREATE TABLE BOOK_SOURCE.PART_TYPES
 (      PART_TYPE VARCHAR2(50),
        DESCRIPTIONS VARCHAR2(100)
 ) ;
--------------------------------------------------------
-- DDL for Table PARTS
--------------------------------------------------------

 CREATE TABLE BOOK_SOURCE.PARTS
 (      PART_NUMBER VARCHAR2(100),
        DESCRIPTIONS VARCHAR2(500),
        PART_TYPE VARCHAR2(50)
 ) ;
--------------------------------------------------------
-- DDL for Table REGIONS
--------------------------------------------------------
```

```
CREATE TABLE BOOK_SOURCE.REGIONS
  (     REGION VARCHAR2(50),
        DESCRIPTIONS VARCHAR2(100)
  ) ;
---------------------------------------------------------
-- DDL for Table SALES_DETAILS
---------------------------------------------------------

CREATE TABLE BOOK_SOURCE.SALES_DETAILS
  (     INVOICE_NUMBER NUMBER(20,0),
        LINE_NUMBER NUMBER(20,0),
        PART_NUMBER VARCHAR2(100),
        QUANTITY NUMBER(20,0),
        PRICE NUMBER(20,2)
  ) ;
---------------------------------------------------------
-- DDL for Table SALES_HEADERS
---------------------------------------------------------

CREATE TABLE BOOK_SOURCE.SALES_HEADERS
  (     INVOICE_NUMBER NUMBER(20,0),
        CUSTOMER VARCHAR2(100),
        SALES_REP VARCHAR2(100)
  ) ;
---------------------------------------------------------
-- DDL for Table SALES_REPS
---------------------------------------------------------

CREATE TABLE BOOK_SOURCE.SALES_REPS
  (     SALES_REP VARCHAR2(100),
        NAME VARCHAR2(500),
        REGION VARCHAR2(50)
  ) ;
---------------------------------------------------------
-- DDL for Index CUSTOMERS_PK1
---------------------------------------------------------

CREATE     UNIQUE     INDEX     BOOK_SOURCE.CUSTOMERS_PK1     ON
```

BOOK_SOURCE.CUSTOMERS (CUSTOMER)

  ;

-- DDL for Index PART_TYPES_PK1

  CREATE   UNIQUE   INDEX   BOOK_SOURCE.PART_TYPES_PK1   ON BOOK_SOURCE.PART_TYPES (PART_TYPE)

  ;

-- DDL for Index PARTS_PK1

  CREATE UNIQUE INDEX BOOK_SOURCE.PARTS_PK1 ON BOOK_SOURCE.PARTS (PART_NUMBER)

  ;

-- DDL for Index REGIONS_PK1

  CREATE UNIQUE INDEX BOOK_SOURCE.REGIONS_PK1 ON BOOK_SOURCE.REGIONS (REGION)

  ;

-- DDL for Index SALES_HEADERS_PK1

  CREATE   UNIQUE   INDEX   BOOK_SOURCE.SALES_HEADERS_PK1   ON BOOK_SOURCE.SALES_HEADERS (INVOICE_NUMBER)

  ;

-- DDL for Index SALES_REPS_PK1

  CREATE   UNIQUE   INDEX   BOOK_SOURCE.SALES_REPS_PK1   ON BOOK_SOURCE.SALES_REPS (SALES_REP)

  ;

-- Constraints for Table CUSTOMERS

```
-------------------------------------------------------

  ALTER  TABLE  BOOK_SOURCE.CUSTOMERS  ADD  CONSTRAINT  CUSTOMERS_PK1
PRIMARY KEY (CUSTOMER)
  USING INDEX  ENABLE;
-------------------------------------------------------
-- Constraints for Table PART_TYPES
-------------------------------------------------------


  ALTER  TABLE  BOOK_SOURCE.PART_TYPES  ADD  CONSTRAINT  PART_TYPES_PK1
PRIMARY KEY (PART_TYPE)
  USING INDEX  ENABLE;
-------------------------------------------------------
-- Constraints for Table PARTS
-------------------------------------------------------


  ALTER TABLE BOOK_SOURCE.PARTS ADD CONSTRAINT PARTS_PK1 PRIMARY KEY
(PART_NUMBER)
  USING INDEX  ENABLE;
-------------------------------------------------------
-- Constraints for Table REGIONS
-------------------------------------------------------


  ALTER TABLE BOOK_SOURCE.REGIONS ADD CONSTRAINT REGIONS_PK1 PRIMARY
KEY (REGION)
  USING INDEX  ENABLE;
-------------------------------------------------------
-- Constraints for Table SALES_HEADERS
-------------------------------------------------------


  ALTER    TABLE    BOOK_SOURCE.SALES_HEADERS    ADD    CONSTRAINT
SALES_HEADERS_PK1 PRIMARY KEY (INVOICE_NUMBER)
  USING INDEX  ENABLE;
-------------------------------------------------------
-- Constraints for Table SALES_REPS
-------------------------------------------------------


  ALTER  TABLE  BOOK_SOURCE.SALES_REPS  ADD  CONSTRAINT  SALES_REPS_PK1
PRIMARY KEY (SALES_REP)
```

USING INDEX ENABLE;

\---

-- Ref Constraints for Table CUSTOMERS

\---

ALTER TABLE BOOK_SOURCE.CUSTOMERS ADD CONSTRAINT CUSTOMER_FK1
FOREIGN KEY (REGION)
         REFERENCES BOOK_SOURCE.REGIONS (REGION) ENABLE;

\---

-- Ref Constraints for Table PARTS

\---

ALTER TABLE BOOK_SOURCE.PARTS ADD CONSTRAINT PARTS_FK1 FOREIGN KEY
(PART_TYPE)
         REFERENCES BOOK_SOURCE.PART_TYPES (PART_TYPE) ENABLE;

\---

-- Ref Constraints for Table SALES_HEADERS

\---

ALTER   TABLE   BOOK_SOURCE.SALES_HEADERS   ADD   CONSTRAINT
SALES_HEADERS_FK1 FOREIGN KEY (CUSTOMER)
         REFERENCES BOOK_SOURCE.CUSTOMERS (CUSTOMER) ENABLE;

\---

-- Ref Constraints for Table SALES_REPS

\---

ALTER TABLE BOOK_SOURCE.SALES_REPS ADD CONSTRAINT SALES_REPS_FK1
FOREIGN KEY (REGION)
         REFERENCES BOOK_SOURCE.REGIONS (REGION) ENABLE;

22.1.2 **Insert Scripts**

REM INSERTING into BOOK_SOURCE.CUSTOMERS
SET DEFINE OFF;
Insert into BOOK_SOURCE.CUSTOMERS (CUSTOMER,NAME,REGION) values ('W1','Kerry
Chen','West');

Insert into BOOK_SOURCE.CUSTOMERS (CUSTOMER,NAME,REGION) values ('N1','Norman Lee','North');

Insert into BOOK_SOURCE.CUSTOMERS (CUSTOMER,NAME,REGION) values ('S1','Bill Drew','South');

Insert into BOOK_SOURCE.CUSTOMERS (CUSTOMER,NAME,REGION) values ('E1','John Ken','East');

REM INSERTING into BOOK_SOURCE.PART_TYPES

SET DEFINE OFF;

Insert into BOOK_SOURCE.PART_TYPES (PART_TYPE,DESCRIPTIONS) values ('Fruits','Modified - All Fruits');

Insert into BOOK_SOURCE.PART_TYPES (PART_TYPE,DESCRIPTIONS) values ('Veggie','All Veggies');

Insert into BOOK_SOURCE.PART_TYPES (PART_TYPE,DESCRIPTIONS) values ('Books','All Books');

Insert into BOOK_SOURCE.PART_TYPES (PART_TYPE,DESCRIPTIONS) values ('New Part Type','New Record Added');

REM INSERTING into BOOK_SOURCE.PARTS

SET DEFINE OFF;

Insert into BOOK_SOURCE.PARTS (PART_NUMBER,DESCRIPTIONS,PART_TYPE) values ('FR1','Banana','Fruits');

Insert into BOOK_SOURCE.PARTS (PART_NUMBER,DESCRIPTIONS,PART_TYPE) values ('FR2','Pineapple','Fruits');

Insert into BOOK_SOURCE.PARTS (PART_NUMBER,DESCRIPTIONS,PART_TYPE) values ('VEG1','Carot','Veggie');

Insert into BOOK_SOURCE.PARTS (PART_NUMBER,DESCRIPTIONS,PART_TYPE) values ('VEG2','Brocli','Veggie');

Insert into BOOK_SOURCE.PARTS (PART_NUMBER,DESCRIPTIONS,PART_TYPE) values ('BK1','Wimpy Kid1','Books');

Insert into BOOK_SOURCE.PARTS (PART_NUMBER,DESCRIPTIONS,PART_TYPE) values ('BK2','RunRalph','Books');

REM INSERTING into BOOK_SOURCE.REGIONS

SET DEFINE OFF;

Insert into BOOK_SOURCE.REGIONS (REGION,DESCRIPTIONS) values ('East','Eastern America');

Insert into BOOK_SOURCE.REGIONS (REGION,DESCRIPTIONS) values ('West','Western America');

Insert into BOOK_SOURCE.REGIONS (REGION,DESCRIPTIONS) values ('North','Northern America');

Insert into BOOK_SOURCE.REGIONS (REGION,DESCRIPTIONS) values ('South','Southern America');

REM INSERTING into BOOK_SOURCE.SALES_DETAILS
SET DEFINE OFF;
Insert   into   BOOK_SOURCE.SALES_DETAILS
(INVOICE_NUMBER,LINE_NUMBER,PART_NUMBER,QUANTITY,PRICE)   values
(1,1,'FR1',10,1.1);
Insert   into   BOOK_SOURCE.SALES_DETAILS
(INVOICE_NUMBER,LINE_NUMBER,PART_NUMBER,QUANTITY,PRICE)   values
(1,2,'BK1',2,12.99);
Insert   into   BOOK_SOURCE.SALES_DETAILS
(INVOICE_NUMBER,LINE_NUMBER,PART_NUMBER,QUANTITY,PRICE)   values
(2,1,'FR1',5,1.1);
Insert   into   BOOK_SOURCE.SALES_DETAILS
(INVOICE_NUMBER,LINE_NUMBER,PART_NUMBER,QUANTITY,PRICE)   values
(2,2,'BK1',2,12.99);
Insert   into   BOOK_SOURCE.SALES_DETAILS
(INVOICE_NUMBER,LINE_NUMBER,PART_NUMBER,QUANTITY,PRICE)   values
(3,1,'FR1',15,1.1);
Insert   into   BOOK_SOURCE.SALES_DETAILS
(INVOICE_NUMBER,LINE_NUMBER,PART_NUMBER,QUANTITY,PRICE)   values
(3,2,'BK1',1,12.99);
Insert   into   BOOK_SOURCE.SALES_DETAILS
(INVOICE_NUMBER,LINE_NUMBER,PART_NUMBER,QUANTITY,PRICE)   values
(4,1,'FR1',25,1.1);
Insert   into   BOOK_SOURCE.SALES_DETAILS
(INVOICE_NUMBER,LINE_NUMBER,PART_NUMBER,QUANTITY,PRICE)   values
(4,2,'BK1',3,12.99);
REM INSERTING into BOOK_SOURCE.SALES_HEADERS
SET DEFINE OFF;
Insert into BOOK_SOURCE.SALES_HEADERS (INVOICE_NUMBER,CUSTOMER,SALES_REP)
values (1,'E1','SR-E-1');
Insert into BOOK_SOURCE.SALES_HEADERS (INVOICE_NUMBER,CUSTOMER,SALES_REP)
values (2,'W1','SR-W-1');
Insert into BOOK_SOURCE.SALES_HEADERS (INVOICE_NUMBER,CUSTOMER,SALES_REP)
values (3,'N1','SR-N-1');
Insert into BOOK_SOURCE.SALES_HEADERS (INVOICE_NUMBER,CUSTOMER,SALES_REP)
values (4,'S1','SR-S-1');
REM INSERTING into BOOK_SOURCE.SALES_REPS
SET DEFINE OFF;
Insert into BOOK_SOURCE.SALES_REPS (SALES_REP,NAME,REGION) values ('SR-E-1','Sales

Rep East 1','East');
Insert into BOOK_SOURCE.SALES_REPS (SALES_REP,NAME,REGION) values ('SR-N-1','Sales Rep North 1','North');
Insert into BOOK_SOURCE.SALES_REPS (SALES_REP,NAME,REGION) values ('SR-W-1','Sales Rep West 1','West');
Insert into BOOK_SOURCE.SALES_REPS (SALES_REP,NAME,REGION) values ('SR-S-1','Sales Rep South 1','South');

22.2 Target Schema

22.2.1 Table Creation

```
---------------------------------------------------------
--  DDL for Table REGIONS_DIM
---------------------------------------------------------

  CREATE TABLE BOOK_TARGET.REGIONS_DIM
  (     REGION_SID NUMBER(30,0),
        REGION VARCHAR2(50),
        DESCRIPTIONS VARCHAR2(100)
  ) ;
---------------------------------------------------------
--  DDL for Table CUSTOMER_DIM
---------------------------------------------------------

  CREATE TABLE BOOK_TARGET.CUSTOMER_DIM
  (     CUSTOMER_SID NUMBER(30,0),
        CUSTOMER VARCHAR2(100),
        NAME VARCHAR2(500),
        REGION_SID NUMBER(30,0),
        REGION VARCHAR2(100)
  ) ;
---------------------------------------------------------
--  DDL for Table PART_TYPES_DIM
---------------------------------------------------------

  CREATE TABLE BOOK_TARGET.PART_TYPES_DIM
  (     PART_TYPE_SID NUMBER(30,0),
```

```
        PART_TYPE VARCHAR2(50),
        DESCRIPTIONS VARCHAR2(500)
  ) ;
--------------------------------------------------------
-- DDL for Table PART_DIM
--------------------------------------------------------

  CREATE TABLE BOOK_TARGET.PART_DIM
  (     PART_SID NUMBER(30,0),
        PART_NUMBER VARCHAR2(100),
        DESCRIPTIONS VARCHAR2(500),
        PART_TYPE_SID NUMBER(30,0),
        PART_TYPE VARCHAR2(50)
  ) ;
--------------------------------------------------------
-- DDL for Table SALES_FACT
--------------------------------------------------------

  CREATE TABLE BOOK_TARGET.SALES_FACT
  (     INVOICE_NUMBER_SID NUMBER(30,0),
        INVOICE_NUMBER NUMBER(30,0),
        LINE_NUMBER NUMBER(30,0),
        INVOICE_DATE DATE,
        CUSTOMER_SID NUMBER(30,0),
        CUSTOMER VARCHAR2(100),
        SALES_REP_SID NUMBER(30,0),
        SALES_REP VARCHAR2(100),
        PART_NUMBER_SID NUMBER(30,0),
        PART_NUMBER VARCHAR2(100),
        QUANTITY NUMBER(30,7),
        PRICE NUMBER(30,7)
  ) ;
--------------------------------------------------------
-- DDL for Table SALES_REP_DIM
--------------------------------------------------------

  CREATE TABLE BOOK_TARGET.SALES_REP_DIM
  (     SALES_REP_SID NUMBER(30,0),
        SALES_REP VARCHAR2(100),
```

```
        NAME VARCHAR2(500),
        REGION_SID NUMBER(30,0),
        REGION VARCHAR2(100)
  ) ;
--------------------------------------------------------
--  DDL for Table SPLIT_REGION_EAST
--------------------------------------------------------


  CREATE TABLE BOOK_TARGET.SPLIT_REGION_EAST
  (       REGION_SID NUMBER(30,0),
          REGION VARCHAR2(50),
          DESCRIPTIONS VARCHAR2(100)
  ) ;
--------------------------------------------------------
--  DDL for Table SPLIT_REGION_NORTH
--------------------------------------------------------


  CREATE TABLE BOOK_TARGET.SPLIT_REGION_NORTH
  (       REGION_SID NUMBER(30,0),
          REGION VARCHAR2(50),
          DESCRIPTIONS VARCHAR2(100)
  ) ;
--------------------------------------------------------
--  DDL for Table SPLIT_REGION_SOUTH
--------------------------------------------------------


  CREATE TABLE BOOK_TARGET.SPLIT_REGION_SOUTH
  (       REGION_SID NUMBER(30,0),
          REGION VARCHAR2(50),
          DESCRIPTIONS VARCHAR2(100)
  ) ;
--------------------------------------------------------
--  DDL for Table SPLIT_REGION_WEST
--------------------------------------------------------


  CREATE TABLE BOOK_TARGET.SPLIT_REGION_WEST
  (       REGION_SID NUMBER(30,0),
          REGION VARCHAR2(50),
          DESCRIPTIONS VARCHAR2(100)
```

```
);
---------------------------------------------------------
-- DDL for Table UNION_REGIONS_DIM
---------------------------------------------------------

  CREATE TABLE BOOK_TARGET.UNION_REGIONS_DIM
  (       REGION_SID NUMBER(30,0),
          REGION VARCHAR2(50),
          DESCRIPTIONS VARCHAR2(100)
  );
```

Thank You

I hope this book helped you to learn Oracle Data Integrator 12c. Please leave you feedbacks by login to www.odijumpstart.com

- Author

NOTES: